Increasing The Knowledge Of
BAPTISM IN THE HOLY SPIRIT

Increasing The Knowledge Of
BAPTISM IN THE HOLY SPIRIT

Dr. Sunday Omotosho

 PYXIDIA HOUSE PUBLISHERS

Increasing The Knowledge of
BAPTISM IN THE HOLY SPIRIT
Copyright©2022 by Dr. Sunday Omotosho

Request for information on this title should be addressed to
Dr. Sunday Omotosho
Email: sundayomotosho@yahoo.com
+1 972 375 6472

Library of Congress Cataloging-in-Publication Data

Dr. Sunday Omotosho
Increasing The Knowledge of
BAPTISM IN THE HOLY SPIRIT
ISBN-13: 978-1-946530-37-0 (Paperback)
ISBN-10: 1-946530-37-9 (Paperback)
1. Religion - Christianity - Non-fiction 1. Title
Library of Congress Control Number: 2022949338

Edited by Winnie Aduayi

Published in Dallas Texas by Pyxidia House Publishers. A registered trademark of Pyxidia Concept llc. www.pyxidiahouse.com
info@pyxidiahouse.com

Printed in the United States of America

To God Almighty, Jesus Christ, and the Holy Spirit.
To my family and all believers in Christ.

Acknowledgements

First, I give thanks, honor and glory to God Almighty – the merciful One who enabled me to complete my studies at Oral Robert University.

I acknowledge everyone who contributed enormously to the completion of this project. I especially recognize Dr. Wonsuk Ma (Dean of Faculty) and Dr. James Barber (Director of the Doctor of Ministry program) for their support. I sincerely appreciate Dr. Julie Ma (my supervisor) for the time and energy that she invested in me and this work, along with her indispensable supervision, great words of wisdom, patience, and encouragement.

I am indebted to my loving wife, Pastor (Mrs)Toyin Kikelomo Omotosho, and my children for always encouraging and praying for me.

I am extremely grateful to all my family and senior

pastors in The Redeemed Christian Church of God for their love, support, and prayers.

Last but certainly not least, my gratitude goes to the members of The Redeemed Christian Church of God Victory House, Abilene, Texas, for their invaluable assistance, encouragement, and prayers while I was working on this great project.

God bless you all in Jesus' name, amen.

Contents

FOREWORD

Increasing The Knowledge Of Baptism In The Holy Spirit is a significant contribution to the ongoing research on this cardinal topic for the Pentecostal faith. The Pentecostal scholarship agrees that their belief in the baptism in the Spirit shaped the identity, theology, and mission of Pentecostals. Their exponential growth worldwide is also attributed to this unique doctrine. With the continuing evolution of Pentecostal Christianity into Charismatic and Independent Churches, this key Pentecostal doctrine has been toned down by some Churches. The decreasing experience of the Spirit baptism among classical Pentecostal believers is, therefore, alarming. Thus, this carefully researched but nuanced study on the subject is both timely and crucial. This book is bound to serve the wide, Spirit-empowered world of Christianity and its mission by affirming the relationship between the Spirit baptism and empowerment for witnessing.

The work of the Spirit is long attested through the Old and New Testaments. The seventy elders all started to prophesy as the Spirit of the Lord descended upon them. When the prophet Ezekiel called the Spirit, it breathed life into the dry bones of the valley, making them a great army of God. Jesus, conceived of the Holy Spirit, experienced the coming of the Spirit at his baptism. On the day of Pentecost, all 120 people were filled with the Holy Spirit as prophesied by prophet Joel. Similarly, resurrected Jesus breathed into his disciples and said, "Receive the Holy Spirit." Thus, transmitting the necessity of teaching, ministry effort, and witnessing is very needed. One distinct characteristic of the New Testament ministry, starting from the message of Jesus Christ through the Acts of the Apostles, was the empowering presence of the Holy Spirit.

The modern advent of the Holy Spirit at the turn of the twentieth century was the long-awaited restoration of the apostolic faith. Early Pentecostal believers were certain that the Spirit baptism was the sure connection with the apostolic tradition. They also continued the established link between the baptism in the Holy Spirit and empowerment to preach the good news to the ends of the earth. And they have done this in the face of the marginalization of the Churches and secular media.

Today, the growth of global Pentecostalism has earned a place among established Church circles. At the same time, this acceptance also coincides with the waning of this distinctive Pentecostal belief and experience among its adherents. Instead of propagating this dynamic tradition to the wide Church world, Pentecostalism may be losing its "salt and light" to renew and rejuvenate the whole body of Christ. Thus, it is imperative for Pentecostals to renew their distinct belief in and experience of the Spirit baptism. This book serves as a clarion call to both Pentecostals and the whole of Christianity to take this apostolic faith seriously. The restoration of this belief, I dare say, has a decisive implication for the future of global Christianity. Among the six Christian mega blocks, according to World Christian Encyclopedia (2019), in 2020, two families (Catholic and Orthodox) recorded their annual growth rates lower than the population growth. Pentecostals recorded the highest among the four, growing faster than the population. Therefore, this book also has a prophetic role in shaping global Christianity in the coming years.

Julie Ma (Ph.D)
(former) Executive committee member of Edinburgh 2000
Professor of Missions and Intercultural Studies
College of Theology and Ministry,
Oral Robert University,
Tulsa Oklahoma, USA.

"And, behold, I send the promise of my Father upon you: but tarry ye in the city of Jerusalem, until ye be endued with power from on high." – **Luke 24:49**

PREFACE

Peter was one of the privileged few who worked physically and closely with Jesus as one of His disciples. However, when Jesus was arrested to be crucified, Peter denied Him three times and even went on to lay curses on himself and swore, *"I don't know this man you're talking about."* (Mark 14:71). Fear enveloped Peter and swallowed up his faith in the Master, whom he had worked closely with for three years.

However, Peter's life tale doesn't end with this fear-filled testimony. After the resurrection and ascension of Christ Jesus, we see Peter powerfully preaching the message of Christ to crowds of thousands in Jerusalem, and three thousand people got saved (Acts 2:41). Yes, the same Peter who had denied Christ not too long ago was now preaching boldly, openly, and powerfully about the crucified and risen Savior. How is this so? What changed for Peter?

The answer is simple – between Peter's denial of Christ at Passover and his mighty, soul-winning message weeks later, Peter experienced the "baptism in the Holy Spirit" on the day of Pentecost as Christ told them to expect – Peter was among the ones who first received the promised baptism of the Holy Spirit.

It was vital to Jesus that the disciples be filled with the Holy Spirit, such that before His ascension to heaven He forbade them from going forth to minister until they had received the Holy Spirit power from on high. He commanded the disciples to wait in Jerusalem for power to witness through the Holy Spirit baptism as promised by the Father. Luke recorded in Acts 1:8, *"You will receive power when the Holy Spirit comes on you; and you will be my witnesses in Jerusalem, and in all Judea and Samaria, and to the ends of the earth"*. The prayers and obedience of the disciples to Jesus' command to wait in Jerusalem for the promise of the Father gave birth to the outpouring of the Holy Spirit in the early Church. Jesus knew that without the baptism in the Holy Spirit, they would have no courage to speak the Word of Truth, and there would be no power to back that which they speak.

Thus, baptism in the Holy Spirit is of utmost importance in the body of Christ and has remained part of the Pentecostal movement since the day of Pentecost; it has also been the driving force for the spread of the Pentecostal doctrine globally. Luke recorded that "When the day of Pentecost came, they were all together in one place. Suddenly a sound like the blowing of a violent wind came from heaven and filled the whole house where they were sitting. They all were filled with the Holy Spirit and began to speak in tongues as the Spirit enabled them" (Acts 2:1-4). The outpouring of the Holy Spirit experienced during Pentecost empowered the disciples to preach, teach, heal, save, perform miracles, and deliver people from demonic powers. As they went about ministering, signs and wonders followed them, and God added to the Church "daily those who were being saved" (Acts 2:47).

Today, many professing Christians who follow Jesus still lack the knowledge and experience of baptism in the Holy Spirit. It is an important Pentecostal doctrine for empowerment to witness, and it is a needed Christian experience to bring back the Pentecostal power into the twenty-first century "sleeping" Church. Steven Jack Land explains that it is not acceptable for Pentecostal Churches to lack the Pentecostal experience. He says that today, the Pentecostal Churches "can, should, and must evidence the same longing and power as the early Church if it is to be in eschatological continuity with the beginning and end of the Church of Pentecost... The outpouring of the Spirit at Pentecost constituted the Church as an eschatological community of universal mission in the power and demonstration of the Spirit."

Therefore, this body of work is focused on increasing the

knowledge of baptism in the Holy Spirit. It is worthy of note that there has been a steady decrease in the knowledge of baptism in the Holy Spirit based on a close study of several Churches. Many Churches, congregations, and leaders believe that the outpouring of the Holy Spirit experienced on the day of Pentecost was historical and that the signs and wonders that followed expired with the Apostles in the early Christian Church. I daresay, this is not so; hence, in the coming chapters, I will be unveiling how to increase the knowledge of baptism in the Holy Spirit in pentecostal Churches through teaching, preaching, seminars, and scriptural resources from the Old and New Testaments, and other helpful literature. I would also be reviewing existing theological perspectives to support old doctrinal issues and to challenge the congregants' worldviews and mindsets theologically, while also identifying and drawing relevant lessons from Pentecostal revivals with general biblical facts for spiritual empowerment, which is a must for Christian witness.

Summarily, it is my utmost desire that everyone would increase their knowledge and be filled with the power of God through the baptism in the Holy Spirit. It is also my hope that leaders, pastors, and evangelists would begin to teach their members and point them toward the baptism in the Holy Spirit for empowerment to witness, for spiritual formation, for life transformation, and for spiritual growth.

I

The Church

It's the same. It's been the same for far too long. Always the same, with the same old clockwork precision as all other Sundays. Even sitting in the sanctuary, occasionally distracted by the big brown clock on the off-white walls, having plodded through the same old routine of mundane congregational prayers, screaming like God is hard of hearing, everything is playing out the same as every other Sunday. Everything except that the pastor would have been in the sanctuary by now if the pattern held true. But this Sunday morning, something seemed different. The verse of scripture the Prayer leader had read earlier still resonates, lingering more powerfully than usual as if that was the first time that scripture had been read - Luke 24:49. It's about Jesus' promise to send the Holy Spirit, punctuated by the phrase *"stay here in the city until the Holy Spirit comes and fills you with power from heaven"* (V. 49b).

Like a strong scent, that scripture lingered so strongly, and as if to further confirm the veracity of that instruction from Christ, it lights up a great reminder of the same but now repeated in the voice of the Apostle Luke in Acts 1:8 *"But you will receive power when the Holy Spirit comes upon you. And you will be my witnesses, telling people about me everywhere – in Jerusalem, throughout Judea, in Samaria, and to the ends of the earth"*. This provoked a profound thought: When Jesus spoke of His Church receiving the Holy Spirit and being full of power from on high, surely this was not what He envisioned – a Church without power.

Thus, it is safe to say that there appears to be a silent acceptance of this lifeless routine within the membership and leadership of many Churches, making it more apparent that there is a decrease in the knowledge of baptism in the Holy Spirit. Surprisingly, many Church leaders do not have real knowledge of baptism in the Holy Spirit, which has, in turn, affected their ministry responsibility of teaching the Word with power. This begs the question – what is baptism in the Holy Spirit?

Baptism in the Holy Spirit has been defined as a distinctive new Christian spiritual experience of the outpouring of the Holy Spirit to 120 people in the upper room in Jerusalem during the Day of Pentecost (Acts 2:1-4). Pentecostals believe firmly in the doctrine of baptism in the Holy Spirit as individual divine empowerment that is experienced beyond the natural human gifts from God for witnessing and Christian living. It is an experience evidenced in the disciples through speaking in tongues and boldness to preach the gospel with power as the Spirit gave them utterance, after they were baptized in the Holy Spirit. Clark H. Pinnock couldn't be more apt in his description that being baptized in the Spirit is to be "endowed with power and equipped for mission."

It is critical to note that contrary to the teaching in some circles, "water baptism" and the "baptism of the Holy Spirit" are two entirely different biblical experiences. Quoting Jesus Christ in Acts 1:5, He said, *"John baptized with water, but in just a few days you will be baptized with the Holy Spirit."* Jesus was simply making His disciples understand that John baptized them with water, but that upon His ascension to heaven, they will be baptized with the Holy Spirit. Thus, water baptism and Holy Spirit baptism are two distinct experiences, according to the Lord, Jesus Christ. And in Acts 2:4, they are "filled with the Holy Spirit" in fulfilment of Jesus' promise. Now, note that from the context of the "promise" and "fulfilment", that these two expressions – "baptized with" the Holy Spirit and "filled with" the Holy Spirit mean exactly the same thing. It is also vitally important to note that the immediate, observable, initial evidence of their Holy Spirit baptism was their speaking tongues – this did not happen when they were water-baptized by John the Baptist. The results of their baptism in the Holy Spirit were immediate and astounding:

- The formerly Christ-denying Apostle Peter, now Spirit-filled, preached a bold and anointed sermon that led to the conversion of 3,000 souls that day (Acts 2:41).

- In Acts 3:1-10, Peter and John, fresh from the mighty outpouring of Pentecost, healed a paralytic man near the temple, and another 2,000 souls were added to the Lord (Acts 4:4).

- The Spirit-baptized apostles performed many miracles, signs, and wonders (Acts 5:12), resulting in many more conversions to the Lord (Verse 14). Amazing supernatural spiritual gifts were being manifested in their ministries.

Now, speaking from a historical perspective and regarding revivals of the 1920s and 1930s, many Church leaders had heard and read several kinds of literature, stories, and teachings on the baptism in the Holy Spirit as experienced by past Pentecostal Church founders, but not from a theological perspective. However, and for several reasons, many of these Church leaders have relegated the teaching of baptism in the Holy Spirit to the background to pick up prosperity preaching and a one-time annual "Pentecostal experience" event in their ministries. This is mostly so because in truth, many Churches were products of socio-economic woes, religious syncretism, poverty, and religious proliferation.

Therefore, with the increase in migration worldwide, the search for economic survival and cultural adaptation in new environments gradually led to a decrease in teaching the knowledge of baptism in the Holy Spirit in the Churches. Because of these factors, spiritual degeneration, complacency, and religious ritual, instead of the Holy Spirit baptism, produced a lack of empowerment to witness the gospel continually. Leaders neglected and did not promote the importance of the Baptism in the Holy Spirit at Pentecost.

For the past several years until now, Church leaders spoke sparingly and gave little biblical instruction that could create a deep desire for baptism in the Holy Spirit within the hearts of its members. Instead, they preached more prosperity sermons, motivational teachings, warfare prayers, and strange doctrines. They created a parallel series of Church events, programs, festivals, musical concerts, and leadership programs, with little or no reference to increasing the knowledge of baptism in the Holy Spirit. Clark H. Pinnock best summarizes the real situation in today's Church:

> "We have placed emphasis on the sermon and the clergy at the expense of the Spirit. We have prized our version of decency and order so highly that outpourings of the Spirit pose a threat. Many

appear afraid of the Spirit, lest their worlds be shaken, and they be swept up into God's sabbath play. So often we set up barriers to the Spirit and stifle the voices that speak to us of openness and celebration. "Forgetfulness" may be too kind a way to refer to the problem. We cannot even rule out the possibility of suppression at times."

In his observations, Pinnock argues that people have placed great emphasis on what is preached and on the clergy themselves at the expense of the Holy Spirit. This is not peculiar to only a few Churches but to many Churches. Thus, it becomes critical to evaluate and measure the existing knowledge of Churches on the baptism in the Holy Spirit and, accordingly, design a plan to support the increase in their understanding as a Church.

Through strategic evaluation, this body of work will attempt to answer the following questions:

1. Will teaching a seminar on baptism in the Holy Spirit increase the knowledge of the Churches on this subject?

2. Will teaching a seminar on baptism in the Holy Spirit to Church congregants and leaders be able to impact many, especially the next generation of leaders, and increase the knowledge of baptism in the Holy Spirit?

One of the characteristics of the New Testament ministry, beginning from the gospel of Jesus Christ through the Acts of the Apostles, was to empower the followers. Passing on the requisite teaching, work of the ministry, and witnessing to the next generation of leaders and to the ends of the earth, needs to take place through the guidance of the baptism in the Holy Spirit. The teaching seminar would involve the Church congregation and not just the workers and leaders, as is seen in many cases.

It is essential to understand that baptism in the Holy Spirit did not entirely die with the Apostles but continues until this day. However, neglect of teaching about baptism in the Holy Spirit led to a gradual decrease in the knowledge of Holy Spirit baptism, leading to the lack of complete knowledge, experience, and manifestations of the baptism in the Holy Spirit during most Church services and Christian programs.

Being an Ethnomusicologist for the past thirty years, I have had several opportunities to work as a music director, ministry coordinator, and prayer leader for many Pentecostal Churches. During this period, I observed the worship styles and theology through messages preached by the ministry leaders. Due to the negligence of these leaders in not regularly teaching about baptism in the Holy Spirit to their congregations as part of the Christian requirement for service, the members' spiritual growth dwindled, and entertainment, instead of Spirit empowerment, increased during their worship services. The result was that instead of spiritual growth among these Churches, complacency, lack of commitment to God, and lack of discipleship became the order of the day, making evangelism and Church planting merely monthly Church activities. Several Churches have adopted conferences such that annual, monthly, and weekly Church ritual programs have become elevated and celebrated above the great commission of the Holy Spirit.

It is essential to understand that just like many in the Church today, Jesus disciples were also weak, timid, and fearful at first, even while Jesus was on earth with them. However, after His ascension into heaven, they suddenly began to speak with boldness as the Spirit gave them utterance; thus, the Church today is also expected to be bold and powerful as the Holy Spirit endues the Church with power. As previously discussed, in Acts 2, we see a "speech-empowered" scenario where Peter, one of Jesus' disciples, having been baptized in the Holy Spirit, stood up boldly to address the large crowd, and thousands of people were added to the Church in one day. Theologically, a Spirit-empowered Christian community began that day and spread to all parts of the world under the leadership of the Holy Spirit. This is an important lesson for the Church to learn and teach their people to help increase the knowledge of baptism in the Holy Spirit.

With this in mind, Acts 2 is a calling for the Church to witness, teach, preach, and promote the urgent need for increasing the knowledge of baptism in the Holy Spirit throughout the nations of the world. This will help decrease the high level of complacency in witnessing the gospel, as well as help decrease the weekly "spiritual entertainment rituals" seen among the congregation and leaders of many Churches. The Church has been equipped by the Lord to minister to the world in order to advance the great commission mandate through Spirit-empowered teachings.

Undoubtedly, Acts 2:1 – 4 was the first and great New Testament Day of Pentecost, but this outpouring of the Holy Spirit's "power from on high" was never intended to stop there. The baptism of the Holy Spirit that Peter and the others received that day was, in Peter's words, for "all believers", not just them. Here is Peter's declaration of this in the inspired Scripture account:

"When the people heard this, they were cut to the heart and said to Peter and the other apostles, "Brothers, what shall we do?" Peter replied, "Repent and be baptized, every one of you, in the name of Jesus Christ for the forgiveness of your sins. And you will receive the gift of the Holy Spirit. The promise is for you and your children and for all who are far off – for all whom the Lord our God will call." – **Acts 2:37 – 39**

2

The Spirit Of The Lord

God's promised Savior, Jesus Christ, had been set to come at a definite point in history to crush the head of the enemy, as He said in Genesis 3:15, and give salvation to His creation. However, God would make this happen by first establishing a covenant people of faith – Israel through Abraham. Israel was designed to be a picture of what the body of Christ should look like when a group of people submit willingly with joy to God. However, continuing along in the Old Testament, Israel was unable to submit and follow God's righteous commands; thus, they continually rebelled against Him, for which He, in turn, rightly judged and disciplined His covenant people of faith every time this happened.

Throughout the Old Testament, God kept reminding His people through the prophets that the salvation coming to them was intended for all nations, not just Israel, and for all generations. Of course, Israel was thinking nationally and ethnically, just like many still think of the gospel today – in individual and new-generation terms. God's plan of salvation has no generational boundaries, and it is more than me, you, and our next-door neighbors; it's about all people from every nation, tribe, and tongue on earth becoming a part of God's covenant people. God never strayed away from the promise He made to Abraham that "all the families of the earth" would be blessed through him. This was God's early hint of the mystery of the gospel because neither obedience to God nor the blessing of God can be sustained by God's covenant people without the power of the Holy Spirit.

Noteworthily, the Old Testament promise of salvation was not only to Israel but to all peoples of the earth, and the promise was fulfilled in Christ. Jesus confirmed this before His ascension to the Father:

"This is what I told you while I was still with you: Everything must be fulfilled that is written about me in the Law of Moses, the Prophets and the Psalms. Then he opened their minds so they could understand the Scriptures." – **Luke 24:44 – 45**

Let's look at the above scripture, Luke 24, in the context of Genesis 3. God promised in Genesis 3 to restore what was broken by the fall of man in the garden of Eden, and as biblical history reveals, He would do it through a Man who would reflect the glory of God to the rest of the world, fulfilling all the law of Moses, the words of the prophets, and the expressions of the Psalms. Now, does this sound logical then for this gigantic redemption plan of God to suddenly become a simple, laidback activity and pursuit without power from on high – the Holy Spirit?

In the Old Testament, David understood the importance of the Holy Spirit when he prayed to God, *"Do not cast me from your presence or take your Holy Spirit from me"* (Psalm 51:11). First, understand that the terms "Holy Spirit" and "the Spirit of the Lord" are the same, and thus, will be used interchangeably. Studying the Old Testament, Walter C. Kaiser Jr. observed that the two terms are applied the same way by the Prophet Isaiah (Isaiah 63:9 – 14). Several important events in the Old Testament happened with the coming of the Spirit of the Lord. In the New Testament, baptism in the Holy Spirit is connected to narratives in the gospels. For example, in the book of Luke and Acts, Luke wrote about the coming of the "Spirit of the Lord" and "baptism in the Holy Spirit", and at Jesus' ascension, He commanded His disciples to wait in Jerusalem for "power from on high" (Luke 24:49). To establish the biblical basis here, we will review the activities of the Spirit of the Lord in both the Old and New Testaments.

*The Holy Spirit at Creation in the Old Testament

The coming of the Spirit of the Lord in the Old Testament

was significant concerning God, Christ, and the redemption of humanity. The Spirit of the Lord was mentioned first in the book of Genesis at the early stage of God's work in bringing the earth into existence. In the scripture, we find that God created the heavens and the earth in six days.

"Now the earth was formless and empty, darkness was over the surface of the deep, and the Spirit of God was hovering over the waters" – **Genesis 1:2.**

In the above verse, God Himself introduced the creative power of the work of the Holy Spirit to show order, design, and functionality to the earth that was formless, empty, and vacant. Here, the Spirit of the Lord came into the earth as God's presence in creation. According to John Rea, the earth was "shapeless – *'tohu'*, chaotic, empty, uninhabited – *'bohu'*" and vacant before the Spirit came as God's presence and as the creative power in creating the earth. Thus, the Spirit of the Lord emerges here as a spiritual force behind the creation of the earth. Furthermore, Benjamin B. Warfield relates that the Spirit of God appears in relation to the "first creation" of the world, "or in what may be called His cosmical relations," and the basis is found in (Genesis 1:2). Descriptively, Warfield affirms the Spirit of God "as the source of all order, life, and light in the universe; He is the divine principle of all movement, life, and thought to the world." Warfield simply says that the Spirit of the Lord came as the spiritual force behind the earth's creation.

In comparison, Warfield likens the coming of the Spirit of the Lord to that of a designer who helps to redesign the present earth in a glamorous way in order to make God's presence known to the world. Warfield concludes that "the outcome of the earth as it is today has been the direct outcome of the action of the Spirit." Hence, at creation, the coming of the Spirit of the Lord was to create beauty and orderliness on earth.

Walter Brueggemann sees the Spirit of the Lord as an "invincible, inexplicable, and irresistible" force, a mighty and "invasive power at work in the world" that is "linked to" God's will and was at work during the creation. Symbolically, the scripture portrays the Spirit of the Lord coming to the earth like a "dove," "fire," "oil," "breath," "wind," and "living water" as the presence of God on earth. It is then safe to say that the Spirit of the Lord came as an active agent and force behind the creation of the earth. Like the psalmist said, God sent His Spirit as a refiner to renew, refine the face of the earth, and complete the work in creation (Psalm 104:30).

In conclusion, if the "wind of God" could create life in the valley of the dry bones, described by the Prophet Ezekiel, then the Spirit of the Lord can fill empty lives and redesign shattered lives. However, after the creation of the earth, the Spirit of the Lord continued to refine the works of creation. Additionally, the Spirit works to enable individuals to do extraordinary tasks beyond human comprehension. The Scriptures confirm several individuals, like Bezalel, Daniel, Joseph, and others, who were Spirit-endowed to undertake special tasks for God. For example, Bezalel was filled with the Holy Spirit and endowed in wisdom, understanding, knowledge, and artistic skills:

"And I have filled him with the Spirit of God, with wisdom, with understanding, with knowledge and with all kinds of skills to make artistic designs for work in gold, silver, and bronze, to cut and set stones, to work in wood, and to engage in all kinds of crafts." – **Exodus 31:3 – 5**.

Joseph was another Spirit-empowered individual mentioned in the Bible during the reign of a certain pharaoh. Through Joseph's divine wisdom, which the Spirit of the Lord endowed him with, Joseph was able to provide exemplary solutions to a series of challenges faced by Pharaoh in his kingdom. According to the Scripture, this Pharaoh was so impressed that he asked his officials, "Can we find anyone like this man, one in whom is the Spirit of God?" (Genesis 41:38).

Additionally, the Scriptures mentioned how Zerubbabel successfully built the temple after the Israelites returned from captivity in Babylon. Zechariah bore witness that the success of Zerubbabel's building project was "'not by might nor by power, but by my Spirit,' says the LORD Almighty" (Zechariah 4:6). This makes it evident that

God endows all individuals with gifts of the Spirit to use them for specific tasks to accomplish His divine purposes.

*The Spirit of the Lord in Saul and Samson

The Old Testament records several occasions when the Spirit of the Lord suddenly came upon individuals for a specific purpose. After the Prophet Samuel anointed King Saul with oil at Gilgal, Saul became a Spirit-empowered person: Then, "As Saul turned to leave Samuel, God changed Saul's heart." At Gibeah, King Saul met "a procession of prophets," and "the Spirit of God came upon him in power" (1 Samuel 10:9 – 10). Saul became king when the Israelites were under the oppression of neighboring enemies like the Philistines, the Amalekites, and Jabesh-Gilead, so he needed empowerment from God to rule Israel safely.

Samson was a judge in Israel and became another Spirit-empowered leader in the nation of Israel. He was sent to deliver the Israelites from the hands of the Philistines. Samson, a child of prophecy, was born to Manoah and his wife from the tribe of Dan. Samson was already anointed from the womb to be a Nazarene and separated unto God for his divine task. As he grew up, "the Spirit of the Lord began to stir him while he was in Mahaneh-Dan, between Zorah and Eshtaol." One day, on his way to Timnah for his parents to ask a woman to be his wife, Samson ran into a young lion that "came roaring toward him," and "the Spirit of the Lord came upon him in power"; he charged back at the lion and killed it with his bare hands. However, Samson got sucked into Delilah's charm and beauty and later married her. Then, the Philistines finally got their opportunity for revenge against Samson; they captured him as he was betrayed by Delilah, plucked out his eyes and continually mocked him, but on his way to the Philistines' camp at Lehi to further humiliate him and entertain themselves, with his two hands tightly tied with ropes, "the Spirit of the Lord came upon him in power," and while the Philistines were still shouting at him, the ropes "dropped from his hands" (Judges 13:14). That day Samson killed more Philistines than he did in his lifetime.

Wonsuk Ma says that Samson's birth was an outcome of an angelic prophecy, and that King Saul was chosen by God and anointed by the Prophet Samuel, stating that both were heroes in Israel. Ma recognizes Saul and Samson as "two leaders who have first and second place on the leaderboard of Spirit-endued charismatic leaders in the Old Testament." Ma believes in "the intention of the Spirit's Pentecostal-Charismatic movement." He wrote the article because of "the ongoing dilemma of the ethical failures among well-known leaders of modern Pentecostal-charismatic movements." He was concerned about the "internal and private layers of (Saul's and Samson's) experience with the Spirit of God," including "an internal transformation as well as empowerment for external tasks" of these leaders. Ma says that despite Saul and Samson being anointed leaders, they failed "to receive the internal transformative work of the Spirit."

Ma continues that Samson as a young man and during difficult moments of his life, had several encounters with the Spirit of the Lord that suddenly came upon him in power. Ma considered why Samson failed as a Spirit-empowered man. He said that the Spirit of God in the life of Samson "was to enhance God's giftedness in him, and to challenge him with the encounter of God's reality to contribute to the process of his character development" and not to become a military leader. Ma adds that Saul, on the other hand, had Spirit-empowered encounters as the first king of Israel, and he was anointed by the Prophet Samuel in a private setting; then, he met with a band of prophets on his way home after his coronation. Ma concludes that the role of the Spirit coming upon King Saul was "to authenticate his election as Israel's king through the anointing by Samuel."

For King Saul and leaders in general, the issue of an inner transformation, or a new heart, is inseparable from Spirit-empowerment because they are both connected as part of leadership. Samson failed in character development, and King Saul also failed in personal and character development, and their lives ended in tragedy. The stories of king Saul and Samson, as narrated, are similar to contemporary Pentecostal-Charismatic leaders. Despite the anointing of God in their lives and ministries, several of these leaders have good character, purity of heart, and self-discipline. Most of the current leadership conflicts that confront twenty-first-century ministries are associated with the problem of lack of character development, impure hearts, and ungodly lifestyles. The scripture records that after creation, "The Lord saw how great man's wickedness on the earth had become and that every inclination of the thoughts of his heart was only evil all the time" (Genesis 6:5).

*The Spirit of the Lord on the Seventy Elders

The Israelites' grumbling against Moses over the fixed menu and other personal daily needs in the wilderness led to the selection of the seventy elders by Moses at God's command. Moses heard the grumblings and said to God, "Where can I get meat for all these people?" (Numbers 11:13), and God answered Moses:

"The LORD said to Moses, 'Bring me seventy of Israel's elders who are known to you as leaders and official among the people. Have them come to the Tent of Meeting,'" and "I will come down and speak with you there, and I will take of the Spirit that is on you and will put the Spirit on them" – **Numbers 11:16 – 17**.

As commanded by God, Moses obeyed by choosing seventy elders, and he made them stand around the tent.

Then God came down in a thick cloud and spoke with Moses, and God took some of the Spirit that was on Moses and put it on the seventy elders of Israel (Numbers 11: 25).

Equally, as the Spirit of the Lord "rested on them," they all began to prophesy, including Eldad and Medad, who were absent; their names were listed as part of the elders, and they did not go to the tent meeting but remained in the camp. This was the only time they prophesied; it never happened again (Num 11:25 – 26). George Buchanan Gray says that the significance of this occurrence at the Tent of Meeting was the sharing of part of the Spirit on Moses to be placed upon the seventy elders, and the prophetic anointing that followed. The scriptures did not state the criteria and method that Moses used for the selection of the elders; however, Gray assumes that Moses chose some of the leading men of Israel who were part of his leadership team. Gray compares the effect of the Spirit's coming as similar to that of King Saul when he met the band of prophets on his way after he was anointed by the Prophet Samuel.

Rea analyzes the content of the prophecy spoken by the elders after part of the Spirit on Moses rested upon them. Rea reports that the Tent of Meeting prophesying "was unintelligible ecstatic utterance," while others "hold that it may have been praise to God similar to the prophesying of Samuel's young prophets (1 Samuel

10:5)." Rea also considers how God took part of the Spirit upon Moses and shared it among the seventy elders so that they began to prophesy. Rea says that the Spirit-empowerment of the elders in the wilderness was a sign of charismatic manifestations in Israel.

Furthermore, the seventy elders received the Spirit for empowerment to prepare them to bear burdens later with Moses in the wilderness. The coming of the Spirit of the Lord upon them represented the presence and operation of God to help Moses resolve the responsibilities of his leadership position. Ma explains that the event discussed in Numbers was "probably intended" to be God's "visible demonstration of the spirit's presence... to provide an objective sign of God's authentication upon the seventy elders to the people."

Several scholars have raised questions regarding the Tent of Meeting event that call for discussion and clarity. Did Moses' anointing and ability to lead diminish after the Tent of Meeting event? Rea declares that just like "the light of the golden lampstand in the tabernacle was not diminished when the other lamps of the sanctuary were lit," Moses' anointing did not diminish. Historically, the principle of sharing the Spirit's power has been a consistent practice throughout the scriptures. For example, in the Old Testament, the Prophet Elijah shared his Spirit with Elisha (2 Kings 2:9 – 15). In the New Testament, at Jesus' baptism in the Jordan River, the

38

Father shared His Spirit with the Son (John 1:32 – 34), and after Jesus ascended into heaven, He sent His Spirit upon 120 disciples in the Upper Room on the Day of Pentecost (Acts 2:3).

The concept of seventy elders continues throughout the Scriptures. During the earthly ministry of Jesus, seventy disciples were sent out in twos to preach the gospel. In the New Testament, the seventy elders were likewise called the Sanhedrin. In line with many scholars, I was curious as to why the Spirit of the Lord came unannounced in the creation, then suddenly upon individuals later in the Scriptures. Nevertheless, Warfield captures the essence of the coming of the Spirit of the Lord in the Old Testament. In a theocracy, the Spirit of God became the main prophetic source through which God has directed, preserved, and developed the nation of Israel.

In conclusion, God has a specific assignment for the Church and for individuals in His redemptive plan to save the world. Whatever the tasks may be, nobody can accomplish the work of God by themselves without Spirit-empowerment through the baptism in the Holy Spirit (Numbers 6:34; 11:25; 24; 1 Samuel 19:20, 23; 2 Chronicles 15:1; 20:14; Luke 24:29).

3

Baptism Of
The Holy Spirit

The mighty Pentecostal baptism being *"for all who are far off"*, as written in Acts 2:39, is consistent with the great commission, which believers understand is for the entire Church age, not just for the first-century believers. Jesus said that sure signs would accompany and confirm the preaching of the gospel, including that *"those who believe will speak in new tongues"* (Mark 16:17). This initial evidence of the Pentecostal baptism in the Holy Spirit is part of the great commission to *"go and make disciples of all nations ... teaching them to obey everything I have commanded you"* (Matthew 28:19 – 20). One of the most important things that Jesus imparted to His first disciples, to be shared among "all nations" throughout all generations, is the importance of being *"baptized in the Holy Spirit"* (Acts 1:5).

Now let's look at some events in the scriptures showing believers being filled with the Spirit — keep in mind that being *filled with* and being *baptized with* the Holy Spirit are two expressions for the same, exact experience.

*The Annunciation of Jesus Christ

During the Council of Constantinople meeting in A.D. 381, the issue concerning the status of the Spirit in the Trinity was discussed; they agreed that "the Spirit is God, as also the Father is God as is the Son." In his infancy narratives, Luke discusses the power and the active role of the Holy Spirit in his writings in the books of Luke and Acts. He begins with the events of the annunciation stories of John the Baptist and Jesus Christ. Since then, there have been many theological discussions on Luke's infancy narratives. Mary Foskett says that the annunciation of Jesus points to the coming of a heroic and miraculous child, who was announced by the angel Gabriel. Mary heard from the angel that she would conceive and give birth to a Son, whose name shall be called Jesus.

In her reply, Mary said, "How will this be... since I am a virgin?" Then the angel told her, "The Holy Spirit will come upon you, and the power of the Most High will overshadow you" (Luke 1:34 – 35). Thomas E. Grafton explains that "Through a literary analysis and study of Luke's use of the Old Testament, one can see that Luke's

41

repetition of the annunciation pattern not only shows the fulfillment of Jewish expectation for a Savior in Jesus Christ but also highlights the need for a positive faith response from all who hear God's message of good news in Jesus." John Kilgallen's view is like Grafton's about the Jesus infancy narrative, but Kilgallen connects this revelation to Jesus' life and ministry and as a response to the long-expected Jewish Messiah. Kilgallen says that Mary's question, "How will this be . . . since I am a virgin?" and the angel's response serves as an introduction to the coming of the Spirit of God in Luke's narrative. Kilgallen says that the same Spirit which will "overshadow" Mary is the creative Spirit that hovered over the waters at creation. The same Spirit seeks to showcase the mystery of God, as well as God's unique act of creation from the beginning of the world.

John Nolland explains that the notion of connection using the Spirit of God without sexual connection had gained currency in Hellenistic Judaism – through the power of the Holy Spirit and without human sexual connection, Jesus was conceived. Furthermore, Luke attempted to connect the concept of "spirit and power" in his narrative as the eschatological "coming of the Spirit" in "the Greek text of Isaiah 32:15" where the Spirit "will cause the wilderness to become a fruitful field."

Additionally, Nolland states that "there is a link between the fresh creative work of the Spirit" in this text and "the total initiative of God" through the unique creative act, "which brings into being a child who would otherwise never have existed." According to Youngmo Cho, Luke's infancy narratives tend more towards the prophetic dimension and the role of the Spirit. The Spirit, through Simeon, bears witness to Jesus and His messianic role and mission in the form of prophetic inspired speech. The "good news" that is preached "through each Spirit-inspired prophetic speech" is not "described as the source of salvation, but rather as that of its proclamation" in the mission.

However, in Luke's infancy narrative, Cho sees a link between the angel's response to Mary and the miraculous conception of Jesus (Luke 1:35): both are connected to the Spirit of prophecy, the creative role of the Spirit of God, and salvation. Gerald F. Hawthorne also notes that in Luke's infancy narrative of Jesus, the same Spirit that came upon people in the Old Testament was the creative presence of God, who made the mystery of His person known to the world as the empowering Spirit of God. However, Jesus' conception was indeed "a direct act of the creator himself such as never happened before in the case of any other human being," and God Himself, under full "control of His Spirit," caused Jesus to be born.

*Baptism in the Holy Spirit in Luke

From the perspective of Judaism, Luke, the physician

43

and a disciple of Jesus Christ, wrote the books of Luke and Acts. In his narrative, the Spirit is central and is associated with power, mission, and salvation. The term "Spirit" occurs twenty times in Luke's gospel and sixty times in the book of Acts. Luke's references to the Spirit are especially noteworthy in these instances: "In Luke 1 – 2, the Spirit brings about the birth of the Messiah" according to prophecy and empowers John the Baptist to "prepare the way." The Spirit empowers Jesus, at His Jordan water baptism, for His messianic mission (Luke 3 – 4). Then, there is the Church's empowerment with the baptism in the Holy Spirit at Pentecost (Acts 2, 4, and 8:29). Debates have been going on around the mission of the Spirit, especially in relation to the doctrine of the baptism in the Holy Spirit. However, different scholars began to respond and debate James Dunn's thesis, written in 1970.

Most arguments against Dunn's thesis came from the soteriological work of the Spirit in Luke and Acts. Scholars like Robert Menzies, W. G. Kummel, John Wenk and Matthias Wenk, Max Turner, and others have contributed to the debate. Menzies explains that the agency of the Spirit is the source of connection to all infancy narratives as they occur in Luke. The angelic message to Mary was Spirit-empowered and was an answer to the coming of the expected Messiah. Nevertheless, "This eschatological outpouring of the Spirit is generally interpreted... as a restoration of the Spirit of prophecy" (Joel 3:1-2). As noted by Menzies, Luke was intentional about the traditional "creative role of the Spirit" and "his own prophetic understanding of the Spirit," and not from the dimensions of miracles, healing, and exorcisms. He concluded that in Luke, "the Spirit functions as the Spirit of prophecy, granting special revelation, special guidance, and inspired speech."

In concurrence with Atkinson's argument, Howard M. Ervin says that more than expected, Luke "stresses the Pentecostal gift of the Holy Spirit for power in life and witness." Additionally, Darrell Bock relates that the primary focus in the book of Luke centers on the Spirit and power. Bock notes "a few key places where the Spirit is tied to the idea of power." For example, "it is the power of Jesus that heals the lame man" (Acts 3-4), yet "it is the coming of the Spirit that allows signs to be performed." Furthermore, Bock asserts that "Jesus and the Spirit are seen as working in a connected manner through the image of power" (e.g. Luke 1:35; 5:17; 24:43 – 49; Acts 1:8; 2:16 – 18).

Baptism in the Holy Spirit in Acts

Luke intentionally wrote his second book, the Acts of the Apostles, to Theophilus. As a principal witness, Luke narrates "all that Jesus began to do and to teach until the day He was taken up to heaven, after giving instructions through the Holy Spirit to the apostles He had chosen"

(Acts 1:1 – 2). From different viewpoints, Acts is an extension of the Spirit-empowered ministry of Jesus on earth. Luke narrates "how God anointed Jesus of Nazareth with the Holy Spirit and power, and how He went around doing good and healing all who were under the power of the devil, because God was with Him" (Acts 10:38). Turner argues that Luke's concern was to provide an understanding of the Spirit where ecstasy is very important, by showing how the Spirit inspired praise, prophecy, and tongues in a community.

Furthermore, Turner explains that the Spirit in the Acts of the Apostles connects with prophetic speech, healings, and miracles. Luke laid the foundation for the baptism in the Holy Spirit and the birth of the early community that experiences this blessing. Acts 2 can be divided into sections: Acts 2:1 – 4 is the coming of the Holy Spirit upon the disciples. Acts 2:5 – 10 gives names of the nations present on the Day of Pentecost. Acts 2:14 – 36 contains Peter's first speech. Acts 2:24 – 47 gives the formation of a new Spirit-filled community. Caleb Opoku Nyanni cites Alexander Loveday as saying that Luke presents the Acts of the Apostles as "a bridge between the gospel and the early Church."

According to Polhill, the Book of Acts "is far more than mere history. It contains much solid theology," which is "found in speeches." Furthermore, there are "many episodes from the lives of the apostles" and "rich testimonies in narrative form for the faith of the community and the driving force behind the mission." Luke narrates the full story of the baptism in the Holy Spirit that happened on the Day of Pentecost in Jerusalem. In his comments on the outpouring of the Spirit in Acts 2, Philip Schaff says that "the entire history of the apostolic church is illuminated and heated by the Pentecostal fire" that fell from the Holy Spirit.

The "Pentecostal fire" referred to here is the speaking in new tongues. John Calvin comments that due to the diversity of speaking in different languages experienced on the Day of Pentecost, the gospel was hindered "from being spread abroad any further." Therefore, God strategically "invented a way" by dividing the cloven tongues of fire to fall upon each one of those present in the upper room. It was an experience of spiritual enablement and power to go and preach the gospel everywhere.

After the baptism in the Holy Spirit, the disciples began to preach the gospel with boldness and power. They baptized converted sinners, healed, delivered, and witnessed the ideals of the kingdom of God, with signs following them and God confirming their words. Acts 19:1 – 6 records that while Apollos was at Corinth, Paul took the road through the interior and arrived at Ephesus. There he found some believers and asked them, "Did you receive the Holy Spirit when you believed?"

They answered, "No, we have not even heard that there is a Holy Spirit." So, Paul asked, "Then what baptism did you receive?" And they replied, "John's baptism." Then, Paul said to them, "John's baptism was a baptism of repentance; he told the people to believe in the one coming after him, that is Jesus." On hearing this, they were baptized in the name of the Lord Jesus. When Paul placed his hands on them, the Holy Spirit came on them, and they spoke in tongues and prophesied.

As in the "Acts 2 Pentecost" at Jerusalem and in the "Acts 10 Pentecost" among the Gentiles, when these Ephesian believers received the Holy Spirit, they too spoke in tongues. And in this instance, they also prophesied. The baptism of the Holy Spirit opens the door to anyone being used in other gifts of the Holy Spirit, such as prophecy in this case.

Summarily, Jesus knew ahead of time that the disciples needed Spirit empowerment to be able to witness the gospel to the ends of the earth, and the baptism in the Holy Spirit, which attests to the presence of God, is a primary empowering tool for missions. Jesus is the risen Messiah, and He is the only Spirit-baptizer who can baptize anyone who desires it.

4

Theological Basis of Baptism In The Holy Spirit

One of the approaches to understanding the subject of baptism in the Holy Spirit is through theological studies. Without a thorough study of the subject, it might be impossible for some people to experience the baptism in the Holy Spirit as empowerment for service. For example, with proper knowledge of the theological basis, people could better understand the concepts of regeneration, sanctification, praying in the Spirit, prayer, spiritual warfare, speaking in tongues, Spirit-empowered preaching, Spirit-empowerment, and different scholastic views concerning the baptism in the Holy Spirit. The theological basis seeks to explain some of these concepts as it relates to the subject of baptism in the Holy Spirit and Spirit empowerment.

*Different Scholarly Views on Baptism In the Holy Spirit

There is a difference concerning the term "baptism in the Holy Spirit" between the Baptists and the Pentecostal communities. According to Jonathan A. Malone, for the Baptists, "the idea and practice of 'baptism in the Spirit' is unconditionally essential," however, "it is conditionally necessary for Pentecostals." In the Baptists' view, the baptism in the Holy Spirit precedes the act of water baptism, which is part of conversion and "the public expression of the experience" of the baptism in the Holy Spirit. They also believe that "the role and activity of the Holy Spirit is a strong part of most Christian traditions."

However, Malone reports Dunn's view that the idea of the baptism in the Holy Spirit is "a dramatic experience of conversion wherein the individual receives the Holy Spirit," and this is outside water baptism. Both Baptists and Pentecostals believe that the baptism in the Holy Spirit, as each one understands it, could happen "in private" or in "a small group" or "during a worship" context. Meanwhile, Pentecostals associate baptism in the Holy Spirit with spiritual gifts like "speaking in tongues or healing."

Stanley M. Horton presents his view on baptism in the Holy Spirit from the perspective of classical Pentecostals. Horton sees baptism in the Holy Spirit as empowerment for service, which happens after conversion. Beyond being a doctrine, Horton believes that "Spirit baptism is an observable and intensely personal experience" that is "given by the Holy Spirit" to "make a difference in one's understanding of the Scripture." Additionally, it is for spiritual empowerment and preparation for witnessing the gospel of Christ to the ends of the earth. In support of Horton's position, R. A Torrey says that "the baptism with the Holy Spirit is a definite experience of which one may know whether he has received it or not." He says further that the experience is a must for all believers of Jesus. Accordingly, Torrey relates how Paul met some disciples in Ephesus and asked them whether they had received the Holy Spirit "when you believed?" (Acts 19:2). Thus, baptism in the Holy Spirit is both a doctrine and empowerment for witnessing the gospel of Christ.

Kaiser explains, "In the grand divine design of the all-embracing promise-plan of God for the whole Bible, the gift of the Holy Spirit was one of the features of that promise doctrine." Kaiser, referencing the Apostle Paul's teachings, concludes "that Spirit reception is part of Christian initiation." In other words, when one believes in Jesus, one is "incorporated by God, in the Holy Spirit, into one spiritual body of Christ (Romans 8:9,14)." Also, Kaiser continues that baptism in the Holy Spirit is a "distinctive blessing of the new age in which all believers are made to participate and drink of the Holy Spirit so that they form one unified body in Christ despite all the denominational or other labels believers may wear." Furthermore, he concludes that it could be "possible for all believers to be filled with the Holy Spirit and empowered for specific tasks at specific times."

From a Christological perspective and Christian initiation, Pinnock believes that "we all in union with Christ by the power of the Spirit are enabled to participate in the divine life. By faith and baptism, we enter the new human situation by virtue of solidarity with the One by whom it was accomplished by God." He adds that the Almighty inserted Himself into human history in Jesus. I agree with Pinnock's view that all believers are made to participate and drink of the Holy Spirit as one body in union through the baptism in the Holy Spirit and with the symbolic Lord's Supper.

From the Charismatic point of view, Larry Hart seeks a middle ground among other scholars on the baptism in the Holy Spirit. Hart rejects S. Horton's views about speaking in tongues as being "the sign" of the experience of baptism in the Holy Spirit. Hart argues, "The sign of speaking in tongues must also come up for a re-examination." Today, many believers claim to be Spirit-baptized by speaking in tongues, yet their Christian lifestyles are the opposite of what they practice as believers. There are also believers who are already endowed with the gifts of the Spirit, yet they have never spoken in new tongues and appear Spirit-baptized already. In Hart's view, the purpose of baptism in the Holy Spirit is to transform, empower, and guide all believers into the truth of Christ.

In H. Ray Dunning's discussion on the role of the Spirit in Wesleyan theology, he says, "We may summarize the role of the Holy Spirit in Christian experience as follows: the Holy Spirit is the life-giving agent in the new birth by which the process of being transformed into the image of God is begun." Dunning explains that the Wesleyans do not place emphasis on the baptism in the Holy Spirit but rather on the work of the Spirit in regeneration and sanctification. Sanctification is thoroughly Christological as the "New Testament pneumatology is through and through Christological."

In the Catholic view, Ralph Del Colle, from the ecclesiological perspective, sees the Church and the sacraments as "inseparable." Sacrament signifies the grace in the presence found in the risen Christ, and it is communicated within the Church as a body. Spirit baptism also "signifies the fullness of grace and gifts" as well as "the fullness of the Spirit in which the Church is baptized." Horton responds that "Catholic charismatics" desire "to keep their experience and teachings within a Catholic framework."

Allan Anderson reports that early studies of the African independent Churches "considered them 'syncretistic', 'post-Christian,' and 'messianic'" in nature. Nevertheless,

George O. Folarin presents the views of the Christ Apostolic Church in Nigeria. Folarin's "findings are that, whilst CAC tenets appear to conform to the classical Pentecostal model, the opinions of the Church's ministers are divided along Pentecostal and Evangelical lines. The official view of the CAC is that the baptism in the Holy Spirit is distinct from the initial work of salvation and that the visible signs of receiving this baptism are multiple." Also, The Redeemed Christian Church of God believes in the baptism in the Holy Spirit for effective witnessing and service, with speaking in unknown tongues. They believe that "the unknown tongue" is for prayer, and it also enables the believer "to build up his own spiritual life by direct communion with God."

A. Anderson, while discussing the theology of the Holy Spirit and the Azusa Street experience, said that baptism in the Holy Spirit has to do with "a personal encounter with the Spirit of God... empowering people for service," transforming and intensifying the quality of human life. A. Anderson cites *The Apostolic Faith* publication as declaring that the baptism in the Holy Spirit "is a gift of power upon the sanctified life." According to A. Anderson, "The 'third blessing' of Spirit baptism accompanied by tongues speaking was the doctrine that distinguished these early Holiness Pentecostals from other radical Holiness people."

A. Anderson identifies Edward Irving as saying that

"speaking in tongues" serves as the "introductory and continuing evidence of supernatural empowerment intended for every Christian believer." From the Reformed perspective, according to Kaiser, believers "in the Wesleyan, Holiness, and Pentecostal traditions have usually held that there is a 'second work of God's grace that comes after one has been converted. Some refer to this 'second work' as 'sanctification', while others refer to it as the 'baptism in the Holy Spirit.'" However, William Seymour believes that speaking in tongues is "a gift of foreign languages" to enable missionaries "to preach the gospel" in all lands and to all people groups."

*Baptism in the Holy Spirit and Regeneration

The term "regeneration" (from the Greek *palingenesia*) is mentioned "twice in the New Testament (Matthew 19:28 and Titus 3:5)." Prominent within Protestant theology, regeneration has been used to relate to "such terms as *conversion, sanctification,* and jus*tification.* In contemporary Reformed theology, regeneration relates to the impartation of eternal life." Michael Horton defines "regeneration" as the spiritual change wrought in people's hearts in which their inherent sinful nature is changed and by which they are enabled to respond to God in faith.

M. R. Gordon describes regeneration as "a drastic act on fallen human nature by the Holy Spirit, leading to a change in the person's whole outlook – a new man who seeks, finds, and follows God in Christ." Steven Waterhouse says that the Spirit, "using the Word of God," initiates eternal life and that He enlightens and builds faith." Furthermore, "Baptism in the Spirit means that Christ places a believer in the Spirit of Christ, and thus, in union with Himself. The union with Christ's life is a new life," which is regeneration. Waterhouse concludes that the terminology of the baptism in the Holy Spirit and regeneration are interrelated and that both produce new life."

Ervin sees personal faith and Jesus' miraculous resurrection to life as believers' source of Spirit regeneration, and it constitutes the experience of their new birth. Repentance, Spirit, and faith are elements of the new birth, and they are critical conditions for the new birth and the spiritual experience of the convert. Ervin argues that "baptism in the Holy Spirit is not synonymous with conversion and the new birth from above;" rather, it is after "conversion and regeneration." He says that "the new birth is the precondition for receiving the baptism in the Spirit," which can be at the point of conversion. After conversion, a believer begins to produce the "fruit of the Holy Spirit," which are "attributes of redeemed nature, and as fruit may be cultivated."

Torrey, in his theology of the Spirit, also believes that regeneration is not synonymous with baptism in the Holy Spirit. Torrey argues that the Holy Spirit may regenerate a person, but the individual still may not be baptized in the Spirit. Rather, "Regeneration is regeneration and Spirit-baptism is Spirit-baptism. In regeneration, the divine life is communicated, and in the Spirit baptism power is added to this life." Torrey says that when a convert becomes a Christian, the Spirit as the agent is at work and causes regeneration to happen, and the Spirit later falls upon the person and baptizes him or her in the Holy Spirit. The researcher agrees that a new heart requires God's divine intervention and Spirit-cleansing for a person to be able to experience God. An individual who has experienced regeneration will physically remain the same person, but he or she comes under the management of the Holy Spirit (Romans 8:4, 9, 14; Ephesians 5:18; 1 Peter 3:21 - 23; 1 Corinthians 2:7 - 16).

*Baptism in the Holy Spirit and Sanctification

In the Old Testament, God introduces Himself as the "Holy One" and "the Holy One of Israel," and "the beings around him are holy ones" (Leviticus 11:44; Isaiah 6:3 Psalm 89:7, 99:5, 9). Sanctification aims at seeing people grow into the full stature of Christ through the Church by the Word and sacrament, pressing on to charismatic fellowship. Melvin E. Dieter identifies justification and sanctification as the primary aspects of Christ's reconciling work.

In Martin Luther's Large Catechism, he specifies "the

ways and means by which the Spirit sanctifies us, on earth by constant forgiveness in the Church, in the eschaton by the resurrection of the dead and eternal life." Sanctification, "or being made holy, is 'nothing else than bringing us to the Lord Jesus Christ' to receive redemption." Christians are aware of the need to live holy and sanctified lives. Albrecht Peters explains that most orthodox Churches, including the Methodist Churches, see sanctification as "a 'second blessing' after the first blessing of justification." Wesleyans discuss sanctification based on original sin and prevenient grace. The goal of sanctification for Wesleyans is to renew people's souls after God's image.

Dieter explains, "The Spirit's work of regeneration of the heart marks the beginning point of sanctification." Whenever believers pray to God in faith to live lives of holiness and Godly love, then the Holy Spirit takes away their sinful hearts and gives them "power over sin." Moreover, Dieter argues that the fall of humanity in the Garden of Eden was the source of sin and corruption in the world, which deprived people of many things from God. Regardless of corruption and the imperfection levels in the world, the mature Christian can still choose to live a life of perfection and be free from the dominion of sin.

According to Dieter, Wesley says that prevenient grace is one of God's strategies by which He begins to move fallen people from darkness into light. Therefore, even though "we are imperfect persons in an imperfect world," we can "still enjoy a relationship" through the power of the Holy Spirit, "of loving God with our whole heart and our neighbors as ourselves." Additionally, Wesleyans hold that "sanctification is the work of the sanctifying Spirit." Indeed, the Holy Spirit "communicates God's own nature to His children," and the Spirit "imparts the life of love through the life of Jesus Christ who dwells in them by the Spirit's presence and power." Sanctification begins with conversion as the Spirit regenerates the hearts of believers (Deuteronomy 30:6; Ezekiel 36:25). The agent of sanctification is the Holy Spirit. He "enables the sinful heart to respond in obedience to God's call to salvation" and "gradually brought us to" repentance, and to "new life in Christ," and being "born of God by the Spirit."

Wesleyans see sanctification as an instantaneous cleansing from Adam's sin and freedom for the person to turn toward God. S. Horton, from the Assemblies of God, says that "Sanctification is an act of separation from that which is evil, and of dedication unto God." The Church rejected the Holiness Pentecostal doctrine of entire sanctification in favor of positional, instantaneous, and progressive sanctification.

S. Horton argues that before anyone can receive the baptism in the Holy Spirit, one must likewise undergo the "crisis experience of entire sanctification as a second definite work of grace" that a believer should receive.

Moreover, putting one's faith in Christ's forgiveness is the prerequisite for baptism in the Holy Spirit. S. Horton explains that progressive sanctification involves the whole person, and it is a process whereby a Christian is moving forward, putting God's will into practice. Also, in sanctification, the Holy Spirit is the agent and the essential means of believers' progressive sanctification. Pentecostals in the Assemblies of God reject the sinless perfection as claimed by the Holiness Pentecostals and use the term "entire sanctification." S. Horton observes that the work of the Spirit in the New Testament that receives the greatest attention primarily is the work of sanctification, and the Spirit is involved in the initial work of sanctification. The Holy Spirit, "through whom we have sanctification, enables us to cooperate with this work by purifying our souls in obedience to the truth."

In conclusion, S. Horton advises that the "primary tool" for growing into Christian maturity is the Word of God, which is the sword of the Spirit. He also says that the doctrine of the baptism in the Holy Spirit is a unique feature of Pentecostal theology with speaking in tongues as the evidence. S. Horton cites, "[L. Thomas] Holdcroft [suggesting] further that the rejection of the Pentecostal position and the evidence of other tongues often leads to a downward trend that ends in the neglect of the Spirit's work on the believer's life."

Baptism in the Holy Spirit and Speaking In Tongues as Initial Evidence

The manifestation of speaking in new tongues on the Day of Pentecost was to reveal God's presence and power after the disciples received the baptism in the Holy Spirit. The gifts of the Holy Spirit include speaking in tongues, prophecy, and others (1 Corinthians 12:7 – 11). Ervin says that on the day of Pentecost, the Spirit's fullness was manifested in supernatural speech as the Spirit gave them utterance. At the same time, he explains that praying in tongues edifies only the one speaking, while the act of prophecy is for "edification, exhortation, and consolation" to the worshippers. Ervin concludes that without God's approval, the manifestation of spiritual gifts could never appear, even at the will of those who consider themselves gifted with special abilities. J. Oswald Sanders also explains that "the bestowal of all spiritual gifts is the sovereign prerogative of the Holy Spirit," and no one "gift can be demanded as of right." Pentecostals say that speaking in tongues is the "initial physical evidence" of Spirit baptism. Concerning the earthly ministry of Jesus, David W. Dorries says, "tongues-speech" had been part of Jesus' redemptive plan to equip His people with power for life and ministry.

In the New Testament, speaking in tongues is an initial sign of Spirit-empowerment and an utterance for personal and corporate edification. With several arguments among scholars about speaking in tongues as initial evidence, Dorries says that after the Apostolic period, "Spirit baptism was relegated to the convert's experience of receiving the Holy Spirit following the rite of water baptism." Thus, "The notion of a 'separate,' subsequent experience of Spirit baptism for ministry empowerment was no longer recognized." Tongues seemed to have lost its significant function. During the Middle Ages, the early Church Fathers Tertullian and Novatian accepted speaking in tongues, interpretation of tongues and other *charismata* as part of spiritual manifestations.

Also, during controversies in the fourth century, Hilary of Poitiers remained resolute and continued to defend the gift of tongues and the interpretation of tongues before it disappeared finally from the Church. Dorries says that between the sixteenth and seventeenth centuries, Protestants "placed miracles on the periphery of Christianity so that they were viewed to be expendable as the gospel gained a measure of permanence in the world." George Fox and the Quakers "viewed miracles to be integral to the personal version of Christianity that they espoused." Even though "Quakers disagree completely with Fox's views, yet Fox acknowledges the necessity of the Spirit's empowerment upon his Church and viewed tongues as a sign of anointing."

However, reformers like Luther, Zwingli, Calvin, and the cessationists rejected the legacy of Catholic miracles as tied to Roman dogma, which is outside the biblical foundations. The Camisards, known as the prophets of the Cevennes Mountains, also claimed to be inspired directly by the Holy Spirit. Their movement is known for ecstatic utterances, including speaking in tongues with the interpretation of tongues. Francis Xavier, a disciple of the Jesuits and Ignatius Loyola, received visions that changed his life. Xavier preached the gospel to several people in Japan and the West Indies in an unknown tongue, and many spoke in new tongues. In the eighteenth century, the English Protestant contributor, John Wesley, set a precedent for later Pentecostals to advocate that "Spirit baptism is a distinct, subsequent experience from conversion."

However, Wesley's continuing emphasis on sanctification as a second work of grace beyond conversion, and a must for Christians, led to the development of Pentecostalism in North America. The unexpected and miraculous healing from a severe illness of Wesley's mother, Ann, and speaking in tongues became integral parts of the Shakers in the early part of the movement. Irving emphasizes the doctrine of the subsequence, that the Spirit indwelling a new convert is quite distinct from being baptized in the Holy Spirit. The gift of tongues serves as "the "standing sign" of baptism in the Holy Spirit, as well as "a great instrument for personal edification. Irving admonishes believers to earnestly desire the gift, to petition the Father with confidence, and tarry until the gift is received. Parham and Seymour believe that sanctification is the second work of grace and that baptism in the Holy Spirit is the "third blessing" for the believer's empowerment, as evidenced by the experience of speaking in tongues.

Dorries reports, "For Irving, the manifestation of tongues for every believer is a necessity. It represents a dimension of practical growth and development in the things of the supernatural in preparation for public manifestation of the gifts of the Spirit." Accordingly, "Public edification occurs when both gifts are manifested, tongues followed by the gift of interpretation."

5

Baptism In The Holy Spirit In Christology

The Lamb of God, Jesus Christ, left the realm of glory and came down to earth to dwell amongst sinners, to be spat upon, suffer, die, and rise to save all; He said, *"I come to do thy will, O God"* (Hebrew 10:9). if he had not borne all these things, if He had not gone all the way to the cross, the Holy Spirit never could have come. If Jesus had stayed dead in the tomb, the Holy Spirit never could have come. As soon as Jesus rose from the dead and ascended to heaven, then the Holy Spirit could come. The Holy Spirit was to be given only after Christ was glorified. The Holy Spirit is the power of God without whom the Church cannot exist or stand; He comes only in Christ, not outside Christ. The Holy Spirit is sent to believers by Christ, and all gifts come through the Holy Spirit. Jesus said of the Spirit, *"He shall not speak of Himself"* but of Me. He will speak to you and show you things to come"

(John 16: 13). This is the Holy Spirit who came at Pentecost and turned Jerusalem upside down. He abides with believers to serve the Kingdom of God and impact the world.

*Baptism in the Holy Spirit and the Kingdom of God

The Spirit and the Kingdom of God became the central messages of Jesus in His earthly ministry. Cho reports Dunn as concluding that for Paul and "for Luke (and his Jesus), the Spirit is the presence of the kingdom: 'Where the Spirit is, there is the kingdom.'" Cho presents one scholar as believing that, "as in the ideas of intertestamental literature, the Spirit in Luke-Acts functions as the giver of life-giving wisdom and the source of the kingdom blessings." This belief is founded on Jesus' baptism in the Jordan River, where the Spirit physically manifested to approve His Sonship and to confirm the source of Sonship blessings (Luke 3:21 – 22; cf. 11:2; 22:42). Cho agrees with those scholars who argue that "The role of the Spirit coming upon Jesus at the Jordan is mainly for the purpose of empowerment for ministry."

During the wilderness moral temptation of Jesus, "it is generally argued that the Spirit functions as the main agent in Jesus' success over Satan so that the Spirit is understood as the source of Jesus' moral determination." Those who believe this contend that this was due to Jesus' early encounter with the Holy Spirit at the Jordan and that Jesus was the Spirit-bearer Himself, full of the Holy Spirit. Additionally, the argument is made that "the Spirit is not a power at the disposal of Jesus, an agent he can put to work; rather, Jesus is the agent directed by the Spirit." However, Cho expounds, "The larger context supports Jesus' faithfulness to God and Scripture as the main agent in triumphing over the temptation rather than any other aspects."

Cho reports about the Spirit also functioning as the source of ethical transformation in the life of the community. However, Cho argues that "in the light of Scripture, it is unlikely to associate the Spirit with the moral life of the community. Rather, the clear scriptural basis for the motivation and source of their moral activities supports human response to God's saving acts." On the Day of Pentecost, after the Apostle Peter's first sermon, the Scripture says that "great grace" was upon the congregation (Acts 2:47; 18:27). Therefore, Cho affirms that a "source of the community's standard life is God's grace experienced through the words of grace."

In the new community, the Spirit functions effectively to help resolve administrative and leadership crises (Acts 6:1 – 3). Cho agrees with Luke that the outpouring of the Spirit on communities and individuals often was for organizational purposes in the early Church. Luke was less concerned with internal life and was "much more concerned" with the community's "outward witness and its effects." This witness often included such manifestations as prophetic activities, speaking in tongues, healing, miraculous works, and the Great Commission. Furthermore, "Lodahl argues that the Spirit is the main agent of Jesus' and the believers' resurrection."

Cho is more concerned about the "outward witness" of ministers that stems from the Spirit. Therefore, not living life in the Spirit is a problem in twenty-first-century ministries. In conclusion, a few things stand out from Cho's discussion about the Spirit and the kingdom. Cho concludes that baptism in the Holy Spirit on the Day of Pentecost, the incarnational birth of Jesus, as well as the conversion and salvation enjoyed by believers are all sources of blessings of the kingdom of God through the power of the Spirit. In life, a believer can experience the Spirit through faith, water, and rite, without any pattern, order, or paradigm. Additionally, more than in Luke's writings, the Apostle Paul clearly believed that when it comes to the life of the kingdom, the Spirit remains the source of blessings of the kingdom of God. Paul clearly believed that "the Spirit embodies the essence of the Kingdom of God."

*Baptism in the Holy Spirit and Preaching

James Forbes describes preaching as an event and a

collaborative interaction between God's Word, God's Spirit, and people. Preaching is the context and central place of spiritual renewal and empowerment. Therefore, "the preaching event" is a process whereby the presence and power of the Holy Spirit "is activated and focused on the Word of God." As the congregation listens to the powerful Spirit-filled preaching delivered from the pulpit, the Spirit begins to "nurture, empower, and guide," helping to renew the life of the Church so that it may serve the kingdom of God in the power of the Spirit.

Forbes uses the preaching ministry of Jesus as an example to discuss the role of the Spirit in preaching the gospel. Forbes relates that at the beginning of Jesus' ministry, He read from the scroll "The Spirit of the Lord is on me, because he has anointed me to preach good news to the poor." Then Jesus declared that "Today this scripture is fulfilled in your hearing" (Luke 4:18, 20; cf. Isaiah 61:1 – 2).

Forbes says every preacher needs fresh anointing through Spirit empowerment to preach as Jesus did. This anointing is "identified with the restoration of power and might, by which the servant of the Lord would usher in the age to come." Thus, Forbes presents Jesse K. Moon defining "anointing" as follows: "The anointing is the special presence of the Holy Spirit in the life and ministry of God's servant, which produces an inspiring awareness of the divine presence. This includes heightened illumination, courage, wisdom, discernment, faith, guidance, memory, vocation, emotions, intellect, and physical performance."

Additionally, Forbes says that the Spirit gives a clear understanding of the content and context of the passage to preachers for effective message delivery to the congregation. As the people of God listen to His Word, they become nourished for their life journey, empowered for service to God, as well as able "to celebrate the present and the upcoming kingdom of God." Additionally, such preaching includes "the resurrecting power of God, which extends itself into the region of death, so that new life in Christ breaks forth." Moreover, when the Spirit is present during the reading and interpretation of a passage, the preacher becomes more intentional not only with words but with preaching.

The Spirit of God gives the Word in due season to the preacher in order to accomplish God's purpose during preaching. Forbes references the Old Testament story of the dry bones in the book of Ezekiel 37, where the Prophet Ezekiel told God that he did not know what to say to the dry bones, so God gave him the words. Similarly, as the Spirit also humbles the preacher to search for the heart of God for the unknown, the Spirit enables the preacher to receive and recognize the Word of God (e.g. Psalm 68:11).

The Spirit helps the preacher in the process of preparing the sermon. "The power of the anointed preacher is to be able to hear the Word from God, and to know that the Word is the Word that brings life in the midst of death." When the Spirit intervenes in the process, then the preacher becomes sensitive to what God requires. David M. Doran said, "through the work of the Spirit, preaching is the means which God has ordained "for accomplishing His purposes." Doran presents research that affirms that "the goal of preaching is the glory of God reflected in the glad submission of the human heart."

Doran observes that preachers face an enormous task that requires wisdom, confidence, hard work, and baptism in and anointing of the Holy Spirit. This need for power to spread the Word is only accessible through the baptism in or anointing of the Holy Spirit. Thus, without the Spirit resting upon the preacher and the Lord endowing the preacher with power from above, all the preaching, hope, and labor will end in disappointment. Doran cites Spurgeon as believing that preachers must have the Spirit's power, "and we cannot have it without the Spirit. This work of the Spirit is an anointing, an unction from on high that is the legacy of Pentecost which ought to be sought fervently." Doran reports Torrey as believing that the work of the Spirit is about empowerment, and it is "the central focal point" of baptism in the Holy Spirit. When one is baptized in the Holy Spirit, one is exposed to "the very power of God" and "the distribution of spiritual gifts" after conversion.

Doran also presents David Martyn Lloyd-Jones' view that "the real object of" Spirit baptism "is to enable men to witness for Christ and His salvation with the power" and that it is "not primarily to promote sanctification." Doran also presents Lloyd-Jones as believing that the preacher should know "when the Spirit is at work" and that the preacher is just "the channel, the vehicle" that "the Spirit is using."

Baptism in the Holy Spirit: Empowerment for Witnessing

Gary Tyra says that the disciples' experience of baptism in the Holy Spirit began to produce remarkable success and visible practice of witnessing from the Day of Pentecost. The Spirit-empowered disciples went out to preach, and they turned the world upside down through bold witnessing of the risen Christ. Tyra calls this witnessing pattern "prophetic, Spirit-enabled activity." Tyra explains that "the prophetic ministry engaged in" by early Christians had "three basic ministry ends:

- Evangelism (bringing people to faith in Christ).

- Edification (building people up in their walk with Christ).

- Equipping (providing the various kinds of support

necessary for people to accomplish the unique mission they have received from Christ)."

Ervin believes that the significance of Jesus' baptism in the Spirit at Jordan was primarily "initiatory." Furthermore, "The only purpose attributed by the Evangelist to the anointing with the Spirit is empowerment for service (Acts 1:8)." The task of witnessing the gospel could be challenging, yet Ervin states clearly that the baptism in the Holy Spirit is for "power-in-mission." Besides, "the coming of the Spirit 'upon' the Old Testament prophet signified His consecration and empowerment to fulfill the prophetic office to which he has been called." Jesus appropriated the words of the prophets of old for Himself, and He "identified His baptism in the Spirit as empowerment for a prophetic ministry."

In Del Colle's view, the divine God-given missions are "the mission of the Son and the mission of the Holy Spirit in the economy of divine redemption." There is a relationship between the Father, the Son, and the Holy Spirit. Del Colle cites a Thomistic affirmation: "The Father sends only, but not sent; the Son is sent and sends. The Holy Ghost is sent only but does not send." Thus, the disciples received baptism in the Holy Spirit as a form of empowerment from the Father and were sent by the Son to witness the gospel to the ends of the earth. In witnessing, the Spirit-baptized believers, through the Church, can bring sinners to the saving knowledge of

Christ and salvation after they confess and repent of their sins (John 16:8).

Baptism in the Holy Spirit:
Prayer and Spiritual Warfare

Luke narrates the story of an angel of the Lord acknowledging that Zechariah and Elizabeth's prayer for a child has been heard, which leads to the birth of John the Baptist (Luke 1:11 – 13). When the seventy disciples returned from their first mission trip, Jesus gave thanks and prayed to the Father (Luke 10:17 – 22). During Jesus' Spirit-empowered ministry, He taught the disciples how to pray and asked the Father for divine provision daily (Matt 6:9 – 13). After Jesus was baptized and filled with the Holy Spirit at the Jordan River, the Spirit drove Jesus into the wilderness to fast and pray for forty days (Mark 1:9 – 13). After the wilderness encounter, Jesus is found rising very early in the morning while it was still dark and leaving the house to go to a solitary place, where He prayed daily (Mark 1:35; Luke 5:16). After Jesus' ascension, the disciples went back to the Upper Room in Jerusalem to pray as commanded. While they were praying, they received the baptism in the Holy Spirit (Acts 2:1 – 4).

In his dissertation, Sun Mi Yi discusses Spirit-empowered prayer in the context of the Old Testament tabernacle. Yi says, "The pure gold used to make the Lampstand

74

symbolizes the divine nature of Jesus Christ, and the seven branches of the Lampstand symbolize the seven spirits. Romans 8:9 testifies of the Holy Spirit as 'the Spirit of God' and 'the Spirit of Christ'." Yi describes the "Tabernacle Type Prayer" as an "insightful prayer" because the people can pray all manner of deep prayers. The Tabernacle Type Prayer is a place for mediation, where Jesus Christ is the mediator between God and man. In Romans 8:26 – 27, the Apostle Paul explains that one of the empowering roles of the Spirit of God is in intercessory prayer: "We do not know what we ought to pray for, but the Spirit Himself intercedes for us with groans that words cannot express." Even in heaven, Jesus Himself is sitting "at the right hand of God" and "interceding for us" daily (Rom 8:34). Yi, therefore, encourages all believers to learn how to pray and intercede for others.

Again, Ervin believes that those who are baptized in the Holy Spirit can also pray in tongues once they have yielded themselves to the Holy Spirit. In reference to the Apostle Paul's writings, Ervin asserts, "prayer in tongues is prayer on a supranational level." Also, "I will pray with my spirit" refers to praying in the tongues (1 Corinthians 14:15 – 18). Ervin concludes that everyone who is baptized in the Holy Spirit "may pray in tongues, as abiding evidence of the Spirit's fullness. But not everyone will be prompted by the Holy Spirit to speak in tongues with an accompanying interpretation in the corporate worship of the congregation by way of 'revelation or knowledge or prophecy or teaching.'"

Pinnock extensively discusses the "mind and heart – study and prayer." The Spirit empowers believers in studying the Word of God to "become persons of prayer who are willing to yield in complete openness to God." Notice that Pinnock explains, "To know the Spirit, we must become persons of prayer." In prayer on the earth, through the Spirit, believers "join the dance [of the divine nature] and begin to experience the movement and interplay of the trinitarian Persons." Pinnock believes that experiencing the baptism in the Holy Spirit will help believers focus and interact in prayer and be able to "envisage a new future."

Gregory K. Hillis says, "we find Origen referring explicitly to the purifying work of the Holy Spirit in the context of prayer." Furthermore, through prayer, believers become receptive to "pneumatological transformation" with the aim of "coming to a saving knowledge of God." Hillis sums up Origen's view by saying that in the lives of believers, the Holy Spirit is central in prayer and in the transformative process. "The Spirit brings those who have been purified through withdrawal from the corporeal into transformative contact with the Son of God, by whom we attain knowledge of God as Father."

Warfield explains that "the Spirit helps our weakness;" "quickens us to the perception of our real need;" and "leads us to bring this desire in all its unutterable strength before God; who, seeing it within our hearts, cannot but grant it, as accordant with His will." In Octavius Winslow's view, "true prayer is the breathing of the life of God in the soul of man. It is the Spirit dwelling and breathing in him." Winslow believes that when one is baptized with the Holy Spirit, then the Spirit becomes the author of prayer. Winslow concludes, "Prayer is the approach of finite to Infinity, and although it is the communing of the spirit with Spirit, yet it is the finite communing with the Infinite, and that through the organs of sense."

In spiritual warfare and through Spirit-empowered prayer and baptism in the Holy Spirit, believers can "envisage a new future" and be able to "protest the world order as it is." They can also "stand against darkness and invoke God's light" by "using weapons of the Spirit." Believers can "pull down strongholds and join the uprising against the present disorder." "Prayer is the evidence of dependency on God", especially during spiritual warfare. "Prayer shows that we belong to a different order of reality which defies the powers of evil and anticipates the kingdoms of this world becoming the kingdom of Christ (Revelation 11:15)."

6

The Work Of The Holy Spirit In The Early Church

The Holy Spirit works in many ways. At Pentecost, people witnessed the tongues of fire on the disciples' heads; they staggered like drunken men, and the Holy Spirit took possession of their tongue – God spoke through one hundred and twenty of His children, and they told of His wonderful works. They did not know what they were saying, but every man in that multitude in Jerusalem heard them speak in his own native tongue (Acts 2: 1 – 13). God does the same thing today because He is still the same God who did it then; He does not change. But the cold, lukewarm, and unsaved people cannot understand the power of the baptism of the Holy Spirit as it appears foolish to them.

However, one of the approaches to understanding the subject of baptism in the Holy Spirit is through its historical basis. In the early Church, the concept of the Trinity received much theological attention through the early Church Fathers more than the baptism in the Holy Spirit. The historical background is relevant to understanding the works of the Holy Spirit as discussed by the Church Fathers, as well as from the views of other theologians. The historical background will include a few Pentecostal revivals that increased the knowledge of the baptism in the Holy Spirit during the twentieth century and to date.

*Views of Early Church Fathers on Baptism in the Holy Spirit

In the early Church, as earlier noted, the Church fathers contributed extensively to the doctrine of the Trinity more than they did to the baptism in the Holy Spirit. In this section, we will take a closer look at different views on baptism in the Holy Spirit and the contributions of the early Church fathers. During the Patristic period (ca. 100-700 AD), the city of Alexandria became "a center of Christian theological education." As Christianity developed, it began to spread abroad into the neighboring regions surrounding Palestine. The Patristic period produced apologetics and defenses against Gnosticism, as well as significant "landmarks and standards," like "the

Nicene Creed and dogmas such as the two natures of Christ," as some of the early Church documents. For example, to defend the early church, Irenaeus of Lyons (ca. 130-ca. 200) published various works against Gnosticism and other heresies.

According to Stanley M. Burgess, Irenaeus accepts the Spirit as a person and as the third in the Trinity. Additionally, Irenaeus believed in the ongoing "operation of charismatic gifts, including prophecy, among believers." Irenaeus also "recognizes the ongoing operation of the Spirit in the life of" the early Church. Thus, S. Burgess summarizes Irenaeus with: "Where the Church is, there is the Spirit of God, and where the Spirit of God functions, there is the Church. The Christian life is an ascent to God, and the Spirit serves as the ladder." Additionally, theologians recognize Irenaeus as a bridge between Eastern and Western Christianity with his placement of "the Incarnation at the center of cosmic history."

Tertullian (ca. 160-ca. 225) made his theology Christ-centered, and "he laid the foundation for a doctrine of the Trinity." Tertullian sees the Spirit "as a gift from the Father, through the Son onto the Church." Additionally, Tertullian considered the Spirit "to be the vicarious power... of the Son." Furthermore, the Spirit "works within and watches over the Church. The Church, in turn, speaks to us through Scripture." Tertullian believes that the Spirit, who is "given to us at baptism" is the "same Spirit who raised Christ from the dead" and will do the same with believers. Novatian emphasizes that the Spirit is a person and writes about the Spirit as "the source of all godly life."

Another Church father, Augustine of Hippo (354-430), was instrumental in shaping Western theology. One of his more significant contributions was "his treatment of the inner life of God," as Augustine concentrated "on the relationship between" the three persons of the Trinity as being equal. Augustine contributed to the ongoing discussion about the Trinity, saying that "the divine Spirit never assumed creature-form," despite the Spirit proceeding "from both Father and Son." Augustine believes that "The very presence of the Holy Spirit is God's law written in the hearts of men" and that "The Spirit is received only in the Church and by the imposition of hands."

In his contribution, Augustine also argues against the Eastern *filioque*, and he does not accept the continuation of the gift of tongues. In line with others, when Augustine "speaks of the unity of the Son of God and the son of man in Jesus Christ, his point of reference is the Holy Spirit," who is "truly God" as well as "the gift of God." Antony of the Desert (ca. 251-356), who lived an ascetic life, had an encounter with the Spirit at the base of a mountain. Antony said the Spirit enabled him with the power to discern evil spirits, cast them out, and perform miracles with signs and wonders.

Ephrem the Syrian (ca. 306-373) said that when Christians interact with the Spirit "in every moment of life," then the scales in their eyes will be removed. Basil of Cappadocia (ca. 330-379) was known as a "champion of the Holy Spirit" and even as a "Doctor of the Holy Spirit." Basil viewed the Church like a symphony, where each individual "is assigned a particular charisma by the Spirit." Hence, they work together, operating in harmony and cooperation with the Spirit as the principal conductor. The Paulicians (Armenian Paulicianism of the 4th–9th centuries) said that when Christians act and behave appropriately, they would receive the grace of the Holy Spirit that Christ received, and they would also take on "the same prophecy and ministry as Jesus."

During the medieval period, the East gave indications of "Pentecostalism," including a "Baptism of the Holy Ghost." They argued that the role of the Holy Spirit was for the perfecting of believers and for "restoring in them the image of God that was tarnished" in the Garden of Eden. Symeon The New Theologian (949-1022) reveals "both the ecstatic heights of spiritual life and the ascetical struggles" of Eastern Christian spirituality. Most importantly, Symeon emphasizes "the Holy Spirit's cooperation in the Christian life." Symeon argues that "This life in the Spirit begins when a person is baptized in the Holy Spirit." Additionally, Symeon says that "One must prepare for a baptism in the Holy Spirit" in several ways. "First, the heart must be purified, for the Spirit cannot fill an unclean vessel. Then the Spirit begins the growth of meekness and humility... and of penitence."

Hildegard Bingen (1098-1179), a Catholic woman, who believed in "the creative and re-creative work of the Holy Spirit," said that inner "virtuous" cleansing comes through "a personal Pentecost." She was concerned about God's elect − "those who have been touched by the Holy Spirit," and people who have received the gift of the Holy Spirit will "necessarily" show this by producing "divine fruits."

*Views of the Reformers
On Baptism in the Holy Spirit

The Reformation Era occurred between 1517 and 1648. Several movements during this era "included the magisterial (or teaching) reformers, the radical reformers, the Catholic reformers, and the English reformers." Specifically, "Protestant and Catholic reform movements grew out of the Renaissance Humanistic reform."

Alister McGrath explains that "Reformation" is used "to refer to the western European movement, centering upon individuals such as Martin Luther (1483-1546), Huldrych Zwingli (1484-1531), and John Calvin

(1509-1564)." These reformers were "concerned with the moral, theological, and institutional reform of the Christian Church in that region."

Luther, "the first of the great magisterial teaching Protestant reformers," graduated from the University of Erfurt with a doctorate in theology, then "assumed the professorial chair at the new University of Wittenberg." Luther had doubts concerning his own salvation. Later, "in response to Johann Tetzel's sale on indulgences," he gave "objections to Archbishop Albert of Maintz and posted his famous ninety-five-theses on the door of Wittenberg's castle Church (October 31, 1517)."

Luther's ongoing "conflict with the medieval Church" caused him to be "threatened with ex-communication" from the Church. While Luther was being kept safely at the Wartburg castle, he "attacked Karlstadt, the 'Three Prophets of Zwickau,' and Thomas Müntzer" by arguing that "these 'enthusiasts' placed the internal work of the Holy Spirit before the external Word of Scripture." Luther argued that the enthusiasts were "abandoning the Word of God in the Scripture and," thereby, also were "ignoring the Spirit." Furthermore, these enthusiasts continued boasting that "they possessed the Holy Spirit," yet "they were actually ignorant and arrogant." Luther believed that "these self-proclaimed 'prophets,'" who "had placed their own human spirit above the true Spirit of God," also "did not have the 'signs' of Pentecost." Nevertheless,

"Following Augustine," Luther believed that speaking in "'new tongues' had been a sign and a witness to the Jews" and that "Christianity no longer requires confirmations by such signs. Tongues have ceased." However, Luther holds that Christians should "expect to receive one of the several other gifts of the Holy Spirit."

Thomas Müntzer (ca. 1488/9-1525), who started as a disciple of Luther, later became a radical reformer who experienced the outpouring of the Spirit as prophesied in Joel 2:27-32. He insists that the baptism in the Holy Spirit, an "inner baptism" that is "the revelatory descent of the Holy Spirit," is more necessary than an "outer baptism" in water. He holds that Christians need to "seek signs of the Spirit's work in their lives" and that such signs of the Spirit "are only communicated to God's people through spiritual gifts." Müntzer holds strongly to the view that revelation is not confined to the past and the Scriptures but is available in present-day spiritual encounters through dreams and visions.

Calvin was a protestant Reformation theologian who published *The Institutes of the Christian Religion* in 1536. He was converted as a Protestant through the Paris Reformation movement. Calvin developed a systematic theology and worked to help establish the basic ideas of evangelical theology in the second era. S. Burgess explains Calvin's views on the doctrine of the Holy Spirit as follows:

The Holy Spirit fulfills the action of the Father and the Son. Everything that God does happens through the Holy Spirit. The Spirit "sustains, quickens, and vivifies all things in heaven and on earth... in all things transfusing his vigor, and inspiring them with being, life, and motion" (*Institutes,* 1.13.14-15). The Spirit gives life, form, and efficacy to nature, which stands at the Spirit's disposal in stages of creation and re-creation.

Calvin argues that it is only through the regenerating work of the Holy Spirit that an individual's "election to salvation" through faith in the "effectual calling" could be accomplished, and most of the time, this would happen through preaching God's word and the Holy Spirit's "illumination." Calvin believes that "the Spirit sanctifies only the elect," just as the same "Spirit gives rise to faith in the elect." The Holy Spirit also enables them to persevere in the faith and illuminates their hearts "to discern Christ within the Word." Additionally, Calvin says that prophecy was an act of foretelling and is equivalent to inspired Spirit-motivated preaching. However, Calvin rejects the concept of speaking in tongues and *glossolalia.*

S. Burgess notes how "Luther contends that the Holy Spirit works outside the Scriptures and sacraments." Furthermore, "Luther calls Zwingli an enthusiast (*Schwarmer*), insisting that he stresses the Holy Spirit rather than the Word."

7

Baptism In The Holy Spirit And Pentecostal Revivals

God is pouring out His Spirit in these last days (Acts 2:17) just as He spoke through the mouth of the prophet, Joel (Joel 2:23), and His people are seeking and receiving the baptism of the Holy Spirit with all the accompanying gifts and blessings. God has risen in majesty and is working *"His strange work, His strange acts"* (Isaiah 28:21), the acts of the Apostles, through His saints baptized in the Holy Spirit.

"For the LORD shall rise up as in mount Perazim... that he may do his work, his strange work; and bring to pass his act, his strange act" – **Isaiah 28:21**.

When the Holy Spirit came on the Day of Pentecost like

a mighty rushing wind, this was His *strange act*. When the tongues of fire rested on the heads of the one hundred and twenty disciples, and they were all filled with the Holy Spirit and began to speak in other tongues as the Spirit gave utterance, this was God's *strange act*; His *strange work*.

This is the day and times spoken of; God has risen in majesty and power over His people – the Church. Many have and continue to see the *"strange work, the strange acts,"* in the workings of the Holy Spirit through the baptized saints, even today.

*Baptism in the Holy Spirit In the Azusa Street Revival

The story of the Azusa Street Revival serves as "the account of God fulfilling the long-time promise that He would pour out His Spirit upon all flesh (Joel 2:28 – 29; Acts 2:17 – 18)." The pastor of the Mission, William Joseph Seymour, was born in Southern Louisiana, where many people practiced Hoodoo. Seymour was a former student of Parham's Bible school. Parham was an independent pastor who taught "evangelical-style conversion, sanctification, divine healing, premillennialism, and the eschatological return of the Holy Spirit power evidenced by tongues." Seymour was converted at a Methodist Episcopal Church in Indianapolis, and he went further in his conversion and sanctification "while attending services offered by the Evening Light Saints." The

Evening Light Saints, under Daniel S. Warner, were "a radical holiness group", teaching that they were "restoring the Church of the apostles." Seymour was also influenced by Martin Wells Knapp, a believer in holiness and entire sanctification. Additionally, Knapp emphasized getting "Back to the Bible" was "racially inclusive, and he believed that individuals could receive "special revelation," helping people know whether they "had received 'impressions' from God."

Cecil M. Robeck Jr. says that several landmark events happened during the Azusa Street Mission Revival. The revival brought thousands of people globally to witness the small group empowered by the Spirit of the Lord. The Azusa Street Mission became a revival center as numerous people came, prayed, and received baptism in the Holy Spirit with evidence of speaking in tongues. S. Burgess includes an article that describes participants: "Colored people and a sprinkling of whites compose the congregation, and the night is made hideous in the neighborhood by the howlings of worshippers who spend hours swaying forth and back in a nerve-racking attitude of prayer and supplication." The Azusa Street Revival "spawned missionary activity in virtually all parts of the world." When the fire of revival came from 1906 through 1909, the attention of the local people and people around the world was focused on Los Angeles.

Seymour had a desire and vision to see diversity as part

of congregational worship. He rejected Warner's doctrine of amillennialism in favor of premillennialism, yet Seymour kept Warner's three ordinances of "baptism by immersion, the Lord's Supper, and the washing of feet." Parham believed that "the gift of tongues had been given the purposes of world evangelization." The consistent teaching of the doctrine of baptism in the Holy Spirit to the congregation led to the spread of the Azusa Street Revival globally. Robeck observes that many of Seymour's sermons "focused on the need for his followers to receive the baptism in the Spirit" in order to "carry the gospel message forward to others. Even if Seymour spoke extensively about the need for conversion or sanctification, he generally finished by encouraging his flock to seek their baptism in the Spirit." Preachers at the Mission stressed "the doctrine of the atonement based on the death, burial, and resurrection of Jesus Christ and the shedding of his blood on the cross." Seymour utilized a dialogue style of preaching that continues today among some Pentecostal Churches. In this style, "The preacher makes a statement or a comment, conveys an image, or tells a story, and the congregation responds by speaking back to the preacher. This is commonly identified as the 'call and response' form."

Nevertheless, Robeck, S. Burgess, A. Anderson, Frank Bartleman, and others say that worship and Spirit-empowered warfare prayers for personal needs characterized the Azusa Street Revival. S. Burgess says that under Seymour's leadership, Azusa Street Revival "participants experienced ecstatic spiritual experiences, such as glossolalia, dramatic worship services, and interracial mingling."

A. Anderson recalls that the primary purpose of the Spirit's work at Azusa "was to bring a family of God's people together on an equal basis." Scholars say that the end of the Azusa Street Revival and Mission was the beginning of classical Pentecostalism in North America. However, after the success of the Azusa Revival, several theological controversies began in the camp of Seymour about speaking in the new tongues.

A. Anderson references Bartleman, who was one of the vital witnesses of most of the events that happened during the Azusa Street Revival, as saying, "The present worldwide revival was rocked in the cradle of little Wales. It was brought up in India and became full-grown in Los Angeles later." The Azusa Street Revival brought people together as one, and "the color line was washed away in the blood." It was "controlled by the Spirit," and the Holy Spirit was the leader in the early Pentecostal meeting in the Azusa Street Revival, as the participants witnessed the manifestation of God's power and miracles in action.

*Baptism in the Holy Spirit in Nigerian Revivals

God is always the initiator and sustainer of revivals.

Austen C. Ukachi described revivals as the "sovereign acts of God that happen whenever God chooses to visit" His people through the power of the Holy Spirit. Revival occurs during God's time and seasons when people or a nation "has utterly degenerated into sin." Classical Pentecostalism had been operating among the people before Azusa missionaries came to Africa in 1907.

In the twentieth century, scholars like Abimbola O. Adesoji, Ukachi, Ayodeji Abodunde, Folarin, A. Anderson, and Abi Olowe have written about the Pentecostal connection in Africa, often including the Azusa Street Revival. A. Anderson says that in 1907, Lucy Farrow and others were "some of the first missionaries from Azusa" that went to plant local Churches in Liberia and Angola. Due to the impactful evangelistic activities of these missionaries, Churches began to send missionaries to every part of Africa, including Nigeria, where Pentecostalism spread rapidly across the country. A. Anderson says, "West Africa, and in particular, Nigeria and Ghana, has been the scene of an explosion of a new form of Pentecostalism since the mid-1970s, to such an extent that it has become the future shape of African Christianity, which turns increasingly Charismatic."

Under the leadership of Odubanjo of the Faith Tabernacle prayer group, another Pentecostal revival emerged in Lagos, Nigeria. They gathered weekly for Bible study and waited for the baptism in the Holy Spirit. After

Odubanjo read an article entitled "Riches of Grace," he felt he was led by the Holy Spirit to invite Powell Williams and two other leaders from the Apostolic Church in Britain to hold a revival in Lagos. On September 21, 1931, the missionaries from Great Britain arrived in Lagos for the revival. At the end of the revival meeting, Abodunde reports that "in one of the evening meetings with the Church, the power of the Holy Spirit was so tremendously felt that some men and women in the Church were swept off their feet and baptized with the Holy Spirit." An article in *The Apostolic Herald* newspaper reported: "Never before has Lagos witnessed such scenes as those which are now daily taking place in this Revival and Divine Healing Campaign."

Most participants who shared their Holy Spirit baptism revival experiences said that "the Holy Spirit was still a valid experience to be sought." Nigerian Pentecostal-Charismatic movements experienced another Azusa Street Revival in Nigeria during the 1930 revival of Joseph Ayo Babalola in Ilesha that shook the entire nation. Abodunde captured the essence of the 1930 revival, saying that several miracles, among other events, happened at the revival. For example, "a dead boy was carried past the venue of the convention, after about ten minutes of prayer, the boy was resuscitated."

Furthermore, "By the third week, about 100 lepers, 60 blind people, and 50 crippled persons had been healed." Henry Dallimore wrote that "People flocked to him from all quarters, and the crowds became ever denser as rumours of remarkable miracles spread about the country." Abodunde reports, "Idol worshippers came to surrender their graven images at the revival ground." Additionally, "There was a mass desertion of both government and mission hospitals because the patients left their beds to attend the meetings, and some were reported to have been healed. Over 8,000 people were baptized in water in less than three months." The attraction was so great that "Many people, out of curiosity, crossed the river and walked down to the town where they listened to the prophet with their mats rolled up, cooking pots on their heads, lanterns in their hands, and women with babies had them tied to their backs."

Babalola, the leader of a 1930 revival, was born in Odo-Owa, near Ilofa, in Kwara State. As a young man, he had a series of angelic visitations through dreams and visions before he started his ministry. One of the key witnesses of the 1930 revival, His Royal Highness Akinyele, said that Babalola was a man who prayed mightily for long periods of time. When he prayed, it seemed like "there were voices of hundreds" in the room where Babalola prayed all night, even though it was only his voice.

The 1930 revival of Babalola led to the establishment of the Christ Apostolic Church (CAC) in Nigeria in 1941. Folarin traces the development of the Church's doctrine on baptism in the Holy Spirit back to its origin. The doctrine of baptism in the Holy Spirit is an integral part of the Church, as stated in the 7th tenet of the Church's constitution: "they believe in 'the Baptism of the Holy Spirit for believers with signs following.'" Folarin observes that the CAC has some of the same elements of classical Pentecostalism that were "inherited" from the Wesleyan and the Keswick movements. Folarin reports that the CAC holds to the baptism in the Holy Spirit with speaking in tongues as a subsequent experience, where the believer is filled with the Holy Spirit for the first time.

One of the fundamental teachings of the CAC is that baptism in the Holy Spirit "is distinct from the initial work of salvation." Folarin observes that there are opposing views in the Church with regard to the doctrine of baptism in the Holy Spirit. However, Folarin also reports that the majority of CAC ministers in his "focus-group discussions agreed that the most significant evidence of baptism in the Spirit is speaking in tongues."

Folarin says that two contrasting views on baptism in the Holy Spirit emerged. The first view claims that baptism in the Holy Spirit "is distinct and sometimes subsequent to the initial experience of salvation, and in it, a Christian receives the Holy Spirit in fullness for the first time in her life." The second view is less supported, and it holds that "baptism in the Holy Spirit is the experience initiatory to salvation, and in it, the Holy Spirit is bestowed on the believer at the time of conversion." After conducting a personal interview with Pastor P. O. Bamidele of the CAC, Folarin says that Bamidele supports the interpretation that "true Christians that have not been baptized in the Holy Spirit do have the Holy Spirit but have not been filled with the Spirit." The person's first Holy Spirit experience is at conversion when the believer "has a measure of the Holy Spirit but is not yet been filled with the Spirit." Folarin believes that the CAC holds a difficult position that "baptism in the Spirit must be attested by certain 'signs', which include speaking in tongues (Mark 16:16 – 18)." Folarin also notes that the CAC remains one of the few classical Pentecostal Churches that "demands multiple attestations for baptism in the Holy Spirit." However, A. Anderson says, "West Africa, and in particular, Nigeria and Ghana, has been the scene of an explosion of a new form of Pentecostalism since the mid-1970s, to such an extent that it becomes the future shape of African Christianity, which turns into charismatic."

The Zionist Churches are known as "Churches of the Spirit," or Aladura or "praying people" Churches that emphasize the work of the Holy Spirit, healing, and revelation that are re-interpreted to fit "the felt needs of the local culture." Aladura Churches began as a renewal movement searching for true spirituality as a solution to a life challenge. The Aladura Churches believe that baptism in the Holy Spirit serves as an essential tool for global missions; accordingly, they continue to grow and spread across Nigeria, Africa, North America, and the whole world.

Also, Churches like the Assemblies of God began to publish, print, and distribute evangelistic materials in other countries to increase knowledge of the baptism in the Holy Spirit with evidence of speaking in tongues. Moreover, in 1967, at a Nigeria Fellowship of Evangelical Students (NIFES) prayer meeting, several people experienced baptism in the Holy Spirit under Sydney Elton, a missionary from Canada and the founder of Pentecostalism in Nigeria. "Elton was convinced that Nigeria was strategic in God's end-time plan, and therefore, Nigerian Christians had to be prepared for the nation's role in the 'last-days revival.'" Abodunde concludes that "the revival was marked by a wave of repentance, healings, and miracles, and a renewed emphasis on the baptism" in the Holy Spirit. Furthermore, they practiced laying hands on people for baptism in the Spirit and for "the impartation of the gifts of the Spirit for ministry."

Ukachi declares that the Pentecostal-Charismatic movement came as a result of revivals that gave birth to the movement. He goes on to explain that the Nigerian Charismatic revivals happened during some "socio-political uncertainties and disequilibrium in the Nigerian society." Ukachi acknowledges that "The centers of the Pentecostal revivals before the 1970s" occurred in the eastern and western parts of the country "before they spread" to the entire nation in the 1970s and 1980s. He continued that "The Charismatic revival invigorated the mainline, the Catholic, and the old Pentecostal Churches, affecting laymen, children, youth, and women." Ukachi concludes that "The Pentecostal and Charismatic revivals gave rise to the explosion of Churches, ministries, Bible colleges, television ministries," thereby "creating a constituency of its own in the Nigerian socio-political and economic space."

Notable Charismatic-Pentecostal Churches and ministries include: Cherubim and Seraphim Church of Aladura, The Redeemed Christian Church of God, Deeper Christian Life Ministries, Church of God Mission, Winners Chapel, Mountain of Fire Ministries, as well as Celestial Church of Christ and others. Notable practitioners include William F. Kumuyi, Enoch Adeboye, Francis Wale Oke, Benson Idahosa, as well as David O. Oyedepo, and Timothy Obadare, who are known personally by the researcher.

In conclusion, as the new Pentecostal-Charismatic Churches began to spread in Nigeria and globally, prosperity preaching increased, and knowledge of the baptism in the Holy Spirit gradually suffered a setback. Today, the old practice of waiting and seeking baptism in the Holy Spirit with evidence of speaking in tongues has been replaced with regular worship services, deliverance prayers, conferences, leadership training, financial empowerment programs, musical concerts, and motivational preaching.

8

Practical Works
In Evangelism

The practical works of some individuals in the Evangelism ministry will be discussed here with research-proven methods, theoretical constructs, and practical applications of baptism in the Holy Spirit. These cases that are presented will help support and contribute to practical ministry.

*Solomon Uche Ashibuogwu:

In a study on evangelism, Solomon Uche Ashibuogwu discusses the role of the Holy Spirit in evangelism, where he identifies two problems: Firstly, "a good percentage of Christians are completely ignorant of how to share their faith with others with confidence and precision." Secondly, "there is a lack of knowledge about evangelism among the believers in the Church."

The study was designed "to assist participants" in understanding that believers are mandated by God "to evangelize their communities and the world." The purpose was "to place adequate information in the hands of believers which is expected to give them knowledge about` evangelism and [to] empower them to reach the lost or unbelievers in their communities."

Furthermore, Ashibuogwu emphasized practical strategies for personal evangelism to encourage the participants and sought to increase knowledge "about the benefits of proclaiming the gospel in the power of the Holy Spirit." Ashibuogwu used the teaching methodology to provide instructions and evangelistic skills to help believers who wanted to share the gospel regularly. This method allowed participants to freely discuss crucial issues during the seminar. He discussed "the importance of the Holy Spirit in the entire process of evangelism." In his study, Ashibuogwu also discussed various aspects of baptism in the Holy Spirit as it relates to evangelism. He believed that "Evangelism is the most fundamental mission of the Church, and it is at the heart of God" (2 Peter 3:9; Ezekiel 33:11).

Ashibuogwu says that the term "evangelism means to announce the good news" and that it is "the act of proclaiming the gospel of Jesus Christ to individuals and groups by such methods as preaching, teaching, and visitations." Ashibuogwu defines "evangelism" as "the presentation of the gospel of Jesus Christ in the power of the Holy Spirit so that people can come to put their trust in God through Him." He says that the goal of evangelism is to fulfill the Great Commission and to "make disciples of Jesus Christ." Furthermore, evangelism is "communicating the gospel to unconverted persons at their point of need with the intent of effecting conversions."

While discussing the historical basis of evangelism from J. Herbert Kane's view, Ashibuogwu agrees that "The Old Testament God is a missionary God." Ashibuogwu says that in the New Testament, "Jesus was personal and perennial in His approach to evangelism," and Jesus modeled the act of evangelism for His disciples to follow. Additionally, "Jesus was prayerful, as demonstrated by His continued dependence on the Holy Spirit and His vital relationship with the Father." Ashibuogwu agrees with James M. Boice when the researcher "attributes making disciples of all nations to making them disciples of Christ" through "preaching the gospel to the lost, so that through the power of the Scripture and the work of the Holy Spirit," people are "converted from sin to Christ." Ashibuogwu is also agrees with Donald A. Hagner that "The universal authority of Jesus is the basis of the universal mission of the Church." "Jesus took the initiative to" train His disciples in the act of evangelism and gave them universal authority.

Looking at patterns of evangelism and past revivals, "The Pentecostal movement has always had a firm conviction of aggressive participation in evangelism and believed in the power of the Holy Spirit for effective evangelism" (Acts 1:8). Ashibuogwu explains, "The Holy Spirit continues the work of drawing, convincing, and converting humankind in order to spend eternity with God, and Christians are God's agents empowered by His Spirit to witness to the dying world." Ashibuogwu maintains that the Holy Spirit remains the essential powerful tool in evangelism and mission. He declares that "The source of all evangelistic power is the Holy Spirit." The purpose of the Holy Spirit "is the evangelization of the whole world. Evangelism is impossible without the work and place of the third person in Trinity." Additionally, the "truth of the gospel" becomes "ineffective without the power of the Holy Spirit, and power" occurs when the truth is operative. Ashibuogwu reports, "The Holy Spirit played such a prominent part in the evangelism of the early Church."

Ma notes that the Holy Spirit's role "in mission has been a popular subject among theologians, mission leaders, and practitioners." Like Ashibuogwu, in Ma's study, he "investigates the role of the Holy Spirit in mission formation and practices among Pentecostal Christians." From the individual process in mission, he sees Pentecostal worship, testimonies, preaching, and prayer have powerful effects in "spreading the Holy Spirit's work in everyday life." Ma believes that "prayer for divine encounters and interventions are where the presence and work of the Holy Spirit could be expected and experienced." Ma emphasizes that "the Holy Spirit is not just helping God's people to survive" but also "empowering them to be powerful witnesses through their daily lives." Tyra, similar to Ashibuogwu and Ma, reports that "Pentecostals believe that the Holy Spirit is at the heart of Christian mission." Tyra explains that "in other words, the faithfulness of the" Spirit in missions "enables a faithful, hopeful missional response."

Julie Ma, while sharing her personal "missionary experiences over the last several decades," says that "The Holy Spirit reveals who He is in particular situations" (Acts 2:21 – 41). Indeed, "When the Holy Spirit came upon Peter, "he became a courageous proclaimer with boldness." After Paul's conversion, his ministry experienced "the supernatural demonstration of God's wonders through the work of the Holy Spirit." J. Ma says, "This empowering aspect of the Spirit in mission continues today." In her missionary experiences, the Holy Spirit helps "in sustaining and deepening missionary commitment," and the Spirit gives a more in-depth "understanding of nationals, especially in winning their hearts and minds." J. Ma sees "the supernatural work of the Spirit among various sick people and the others as it relates to" the role of the Spirit in mission. As in the book of Acts, J. Ma declares, "It is the Spirit of God that leads His people to undertake His mission in the world."

To achieve the objectives of his study, Ashibuogwu "designed and implemented a two-day teaching seminar with ten selected participants" from the Church. The workshop addressed areas where the participants were "lacking in knowledge," which empowered them "to share the love of Jesus to the lost in their communities."

Ashibuogwu "concluded that conducting seminars through teaching impacted the believers and increased their knowledge of evangelism" and the importance of the work of the Holy Spirit in witnessing the gospel.

*Jeong Yeol Ha:

Jeong Yeol Ha conducted his Doctor of Ministry project at Yoido Full Gospel Church (YFGC) Yoido-dong in Seoul. In 1992, Ha was ordained as an elder at the Church. The Church, "with a membership of 750,000," became "the origin of the Korean Pentecostal Movement" and "the largest Church in the world." The Church became a place where the "works of the Holy Spirit have become the driving force for the maturation of individual Christians, for Church growth, and for leading the Holy Spirit movement among other denominations." The purpose of Ha's research was "to suggest a way to further the expansion of the ceaseless experience of spiritual gifts, through systematic education of Pentecostal understanding of baptism in the Holy Spirit."

YFGC began when Yong-gi Cho, Ja-sil Choi, and five other Church members held their first service on May 18, 1958." Ha believes that "The essence of the Pentecostal Holy Spirit Movement is to be baptized in the Holy Spirit" with signs through "believers who are regenerated for eschatological evangelization" and through "various gifts that are initiated by and occur from the Holy Spirit." One of the main problems related by Ha "is that there is a tendency in YFGC that various spiritual gifts, which have manifested among the lay people, diminish or disappear," and Ha attributes this to "a lack of understanding of baptism in the Holy Spirit and a lack of passion for the gifts of the Holy Spirit."

These spiritual gifts, which formed the bedrock of the Church, became less frequent and "virtually disappeared in the rapidly changing situation of the ministry," where "baptism in the Holy Spirit and the accompanying experience of spiritual gifts, appear as 'formulized and normative patterns' (Acts 1:4 – 8, 2:1 – 4, Mark 16:16 – 18, 1 Corinthians 12:7, 13)." Ha discusses the difference between understanding the baptism in the Holy Spirit and understanding spiritual gifts in order "to increase the motives for spiritual gifts, which are accompanied by baptism in the Holy Spirit, which is itself given to believers." Ha's project was "a key for the expansion" of the Holy Spirit's movement, "the revival of the Church," and to "raise the status of YFGC."

Ha defines "baptism in the Holy Spirit" as an "event in which we directly experience the Holy Spirit, who enlightens us to the purpose of 'baptism in the Holy Spirit.'" It was "performed by Jesus" after His ascension, and "it has continued up until the present day, throughout the entire history of the Church." Additionally, "the gifts of the Holy Spirit" "are the gifts of God which empower us in order that we may serve and work for the Lord," and the gifts are "the expression of the grace and power of God." Spiritual gifts cannot exist "without the Holy Spirit, and nobody can acquire spiritual gifts as an individual possession." "The fullness of the Holy Spirit," according to Ha, "indicates the state" of having been "filled with the Holy Spirit as the result of baptism in the Holy Spirit (Acts 2:1 – 4; 4:8; 4:31; 7:55; 9:17)." Ha argues that Christians who have been "baptized in the Holy Spirit will normally experience spiritual gifts."

Ha's methodology includes a sample group who have been members of YFGC for "more than three years and have received water baptism, but whose spiritual levels" differ from others. These members already had significant "influence among the Pentecostal Churches" and already had "a pre-understanding of the baptism in the Holy Spirit and spiritual gifts." Ha organized a ten-week systematic educational training program for the participants. It focused on the students' experiences in real life and spiritual growth, to enable them to experience spiritual gifts based on the Scriptures. Ha's research hypotheses include that if the people were trained in this program, "they will experience speaking in tongues." Due to their change of thinking on baptism in the Holy Spirit and spiritual gifts, they will be able to "evangelize as passionate witnesses," and "they will mature in their prayer life and meditation on the Bible."

Ha's rationale for the research is that "Some Christians who do not have a biblical basis on baptism in the Holy Spirit are under a misconception that the gifts of the Holy Spirit came only upon special people, by special grace." He researched "relative articles and practical examples" that led to "the rationale and procedure" for his research "by giving instructions and programs" that he developed. Other resources included lecture notes, study teaching materials, sermons, Bible study notes, lecture series, and other similar projects. Ha emphasized "direct and individual experience through powerful motivation." He cited some cases in the book of Acts to show that many had misunderstood or had never heard about the baptism in the Holy Spirit in order to resolve some problems about the subject and support his research. In his teaching, Ha also utilized "praise, unison prayer, and home study" as channels "to experience spiritual gifts."

Ha designed and prepared "home study teaching materials," as well as cassette tapes on Spirit baptism. He utilized "prayer meetings," "practices and testimonies" to "go side by side" as auxiliary elements. Ha encouraged participants "to listen to Yong-gi Cho's cassette tapes." For believers to seek for the fullness of the Spirit through the "laying of hands by pastors," participants were required to attend the Friday Night Prayer services during the training period. Ha used the Church members for the training, and he selected fifteen lay people as the sample population. He makes use of both independent and dependent variables. Participants also received application forms for the ten-week (70-days) seminar, and he provided the necessary tools for the seminar.

Ha's research place emphasis on baptism in the Holy Spirit as established in the New Testament. He said that in both the Old Testament and New Testament experiences, God revealed Himself through the same gifts of the Holy Spirit. The experiences of the Spirit of the Lord in the Old Testament became the source of empowerment for service and knowing God through events and covenants. For example, in the Old Testament, the Spirit of the Lord came upon selected leaders and certain prophets to empower them to speak and serve the people. Ha said, "Won-suk Ma notes that 'the Spirit of God that came upon the prophets is one basis of the charismatic pneumatology of the New Testament.'" Ha believes that the gifts of the Spirit of God that came upon the prophets neither belong to an individual nor are controlled by an individual.

Ha said, "One of the purposes of experiencing God is to let us know that God is the LORD of Israel, and Israel is the people of God (Exodus 6:7, 10:2)." Furthermore, "The experience of God," shown in the prophecies (e.g., Joel 2:28), came to be "fulfilled on the day of Pentecost" through the baptism in the Holy Spirit (John 14:20). Additionally, the Day of Pentecost event, which was the fulfillment of Old Testament prophecy, brought a "new era of the Holy Spirit with supernatural and spiritual phenomena accompanied by baptism in the Holy Spirit" (Acts 2:1 – 33). Ha references Ervin as supporting Ha's stance that "Christians who experienced the Pentecost event and a life of fullness of the Holy Spirit in their community made a difference with a simple propositional approach."

It is agreeable with Ha that baptism in the Holy Spirit is a source of "supernatural empowerment for world evangelization" (Acts 1:8; Luke 24:49). In baptism in the Holy Spirit, believers "were all baptized by one Spirit into one body (1 Corinthians 12:13)." The believer's old self that died with Christ is already "buried in the Holy Spirit." This indicates burial and circumcision through Christ. Not only that, as the Spirit is poured out, a new heart is given to replace a stone heart (Romans 5:5; 6:4; Colossians 2:12; Joel 2:28; Ezekiel 36:26). Ha argues that "regeneration is not baptism in the Holy Spirit." It is quite agreeable that there is a difference between baptism in the Holy Spirit and water baptism. Ha explains,

"The executor of water baptism is 'man,' and the one who receives water baptism is in the water." The executor of Spirit baptism is Jesus, "and He submerged Christians into the Holy Spirit (Matthew 3:11)." Ha also explains that "there is a difference between baptism in the Holy Spirit and fullness of the Holy Spirit" (John 1:33; Acts 1:5; 2:1 – 4).

Ha concludes that without Spirit baptism, "there cannot be the fullness of the Holy Spirit, and there can be no baptism in the Holy Spirit without the fullness of the Holy Spirit." As part of Ha's project, he chose Acts 2 as the biblical basis for the outpouring of baptism in the Holy Spirit and the spiritual gifts on the Day of Pentecost. Ha cites F. F. Bruce's, J. Rodman Williams', and Gordon Fee's contributions to Spirit baptism experiences in the Acts of Apostles and the Epistles. Ha notes that these scholars discuss the Spirit baptism experiences of different people from various backgrounds: in Samaria (Acts 8:15 – 20), Paul (Acts 9:17 – 18), Cornelius (Acts 10:44 – 46), and Ephesus (Acts 19:1 – 6). From these passages, Ha identifies some commonalities: forgiveness of sin and teaching on baptism in the Holy Spirit; water baptism "before receiving the baptism in the Holy Spirit;" and the baptism in the Holy Spirit accompanied with spiritual gifts.

Ha holds that the coming of the Holy Spirit and Spirit baptism accompanied by spiritual gifts are the fulfillment of a new covenant (Acts 1:5 – 8). He says that the baptism in the Holy Spirit experienced on the Day of Pentecost continues till today and has never ceased. Ha reports, "Ervin asserts that the Pentecostal baptism in and fullness of the Spirit is not confounded with the Holy Spirit's activity in conversion."

Ha presents Luke discussing "power for service" and "being filled with the Holy Spirit" several times in his writings. Ha agrees with Luke's theology that "the Holy Spirit who accompanies various gifts and works in the Church is the same Spirit who worked in the ministry of Jesus." The two "purposes of baptism in the Holy Spirit are to be a witness who has power and to experience becoming a witness of the Gospel." Ha explains that "baptism in the Holy Spirit is a motive, a divine preparation, and a plan, which provides urgency and power." Ha believes, based on Peter's Spirit-empowered sermons in Acts 2, that "the promise of the Father" became the foundation for "the coming of the Holy Spirit and the accompanying experience of spiritual gifts" (Acts 2:33). The supernatural and charismatic phenomena that are accompanied by baptism in the Holy Spirit "are a formal experience of all people in the Apostolic Church."

Ha concludes that "the era of salvation began with the new works of the Holy Spirit." The two-fold ministry of the Holy Spirit includes "the work of regeneration" and "the work of baptism in the Holy Spirit". Ha relates, "Baptism in the Holy Spirit is subsequent to the work of regeneration and is an additional work." A believer may be regenerated but might not have received the baptism in the Holy Spirit. All Christians "have the Holy Spirit, but not all of them" have received the "baptism in the Holy Spirit."

*Gbolahan Olukayode Akinsanya:

Akinsanya states, "The Pentecostal self-understanding of power in mission" is established in Acts 1:8. He believes that "without divine empowerment and enablement," disciples will not be able to accomplish the great commission that was given to them by Jesus Christ. Akinsanya explains that the "experience of divine power for mission in the world by Christians is the central task at hand." Akinsanya described "power" as "a spiritual reality that is associated with God over any kind of power which is natural, worldly, social, political, or economic in nature." He examines the Pentecostal movement within the Nigerian context and focuses "on the history of the establishment of the Pentecostal mission" therein. Akinsanya undertook understanding "how Christians were empowered for mission in the Nigerian context."

Akinsanya explains, "The concept of power in mission" has always been central to Lucan theology, as well as a "key concept" in the New Testament. Akinsanya says that from the historical perspective of Christian missions, at different times, people have always been powerful tools in witnessing the life and ministry of Jesus Christ. From the Luke-Acts narrative, Akinsanya reports that the early new Christian Church "was founded on the experience of the power of the Spirit." They were also "empowered to bear witness to the life, ministry, death, and resurrection of Christ in the context of their world." Akinsanya's research examines the historical trend as a result of the continuous "growth of Christianity in sub-Saharan Africa," which was becoming "central to the shape and the form of global Christianity."

Akinsanya mentions some "factors that led to the birth," establishment, "and growth" of the Pentecostal movement in Nigeria. In 1901, a new modern Pentecostal movement had begun in the United States of America, and this spread to Nigeria and other parts of Africa, which led to the establishment of "the Apostolic Church of Nigeria" (1918). Additionally, several prayer movements began "within and outside the mainline Christian denominations." Other factors included the impact of the Aladura prayer group movement, which grew rapidly in Southwestern Nigeria. The zeal for power among the Nigerian Christian Pentecostal movements also led to the birth and the development of the Pentecostal mission in the Nigerian context.

Akinsanya notes, "The Pentecostal movement has been largely interpreted, both within and without, in terms of its most characteristic feature, glossolalia, or 'speaking in tongues.'" He observes that there is a similarity between the African religions and the modern Pentecostal movement. Akinsanya says that both groups have a central yearning for divine empowerment, enablement experiences, and wanting to gain access to it. Africans then "recognized and acknowledged" that divine power comes only through Jesus Christ. Akinsanya's research methodology included an inquiry and a critical historical analysis into "the rise and early development of the Pentecostal movement in Nigeria."

According to Akinsanya, Nigerians "were active participants in the establishment of the Pentecostal mission and... their understanding of the receipt of divine power is crucial and also central to the understanding of the history of the Nigerian Pentecostal mission." Akinsanya observes that ceaseless prayers across parts of Nigeria had played a dominant role in the rise of the Aladura movement and other forerunners of the Pentecostal movement in the region. Regardless of differences in Nigerian cultures and traditions, prayer is vital among the people of Nigeria. Prayer serves as a "meditation between human beings and the supernatural realm." Prayer is a means of approaching God in "worship, praise, thanksgiving, supplications, and petitions." Prayer is a significant "link between the visible and the invisible realm," "the natural world and world of the spirits," "between human beings and God," the Creator. Nigerians believe in intercessory prayers on behalf of the people, as well as "kings, chiefs, priests, and priestesses, heads of lineages, heads of family," and the community at large.

Akinsanya connects "the advent of mainline Christianity in Nigeria" back to the Day of Pentecost in Acts 2. He says, "There is no doubt that many of the Jews and proselytes who heard the preaching of the gospel" on the day of Pentecost had come from Egypt and parts of Libya adjoining Cyrene in parts of northern Africa (Acts 2:10). One of the prayer groups that was formed during "the classical Pentecostal movement in Nigeria" is Faith Tabernacle. This Aladura prayer group seeks the restoration of the New Testament power. They study and desire through prayer "to experience the supernatural power of God," that is the baptism in the Holy Spirit "that they heard preached and read from the Bible."

Akinsanya further explains:

> There is an essential continuity between the Nigeria religio-cultural need for access to the supernatural power of God through prayer in order to put that power to work in meeting human needs and solving human problems and the Pentecostal message that divine power is immediately available and mediated through the Holy Spirit. Here the dynamic link between prayer and divine healing

was central to the birth of the Pentecostal movement in the Nigerian context.

Akinsanya traced revivals as an important historical source of development of the Pentecostal movement in Nigeria. He cites the revival that took place at St. Paul's Anglican Church, Breadfruit Street, in Lagos. Bishop James Johnson conducted the revival. "Johnson preached on the baptism in the Holy Spirit for believers and the efficacy of prayer by believers through faith in the name of Jesus Christ." Akinsanya refers to the great revival of 1930 that happened in Western Nigeria under Joseph Ayo Babalola. The revival was a "demonstration of God's power," which they had never experienced in the mainline Christian Churches. R. A. Torrey, like Akinsanya, believes that there is a link between the efficacy of prayer and God's power.

Torrey explains:

> All things being equal, your growth and mine into the likeness of our Lord and Savior, Jesus Christ, will be in exact proportion to the time and heart we put into prayer. Prayer not only promotes personal holiness, but prayer will also bring the power of God into our work. The power of God is ours to have if we will only seek it by prayer, for any and every line of service God calls us to.

In conclusion, Akinsanya also discussed Spirit and power, the efficacy of prayers, intercessory prayers, and the baptism in the Holy Spirit as a means to receive God's power in our lives. Akinsanya said that Nigerian Pentecostal believers continued to wait through faith and prayer to receive the power of God through baptism in the Holy Spirit.

*Michael Stafford Baynes Reid:

Reid's Doctor of Ministry project focused more on spiritual warfare. Reid's purpose was "to measure and assess the impact of teaching a course on 'spiritual warfare' to a population of pastors and Church leaders." The research problem was that "The traditional teaching on spiritual warfare in most evangelical Churches until about twenty years ago was based on Ephesians 6. It was taught as part of fundamental Church doctrine, and believers were enjoined to put on the whole armour of God in order to stand against the wiles of the devil." The setting of the project was at Peniel Pentecostal Church, which Reid established in November 1976. Reid hypothesized that "the exposition of biblical and theological truth, applied in both historical and a modern context, with opportunity for study, discussion, and re-evaluation of relevant concepts, would ensure that the understanding and practice of spiritual warfare was brought into alignment with the Word of God."

Reid defines the term "territorial spirits" as demons that "have been assigned to specific geographical areas," and he defines "warfare prayer" as "the chief weapon for engaging the enemy in battle and aims to overcome the resistance of the evil powers to God's will." Thus, warfare prayer is "a high volume, high energy, prolonged challenge to taunt the spirits until they manifest in one way or another." "Spiritual mapping," which involves "spiritual discernment," is an "attempt to see a city or a nation or the world as it really is, not as it appears to be." Spiritual mapping "includes discovering the location of demons, their activities, their names, and their power." Reid traced the biblical basis for spiritual warfare and its origin back to the Old Testament.

Reid explains that "the location and nature of the battle" began in the Garden of Eden with Adam and Eve after they disobeyed God's instruction. Reid believes that the spiritual warfare "battlefield is in the mind." He holds that the only weapon of Satan is deception, and his single "sphere of operation is that which God permits within His own eternal purposes." In the New Testament, Reid reports that after humankind fell in the Garden of Eden, Jesus came to earth to restore humanity to its original position. During Jesus' earthly ministry, several clashes took place between Him and the spiritual powers. Reid reports that the Scripture "records that Jesus 'preached in their synagogues throughout all Galilee and cast out devils' (Mark 1:39)." Reid explains that

Jesus, being "the incarnate Word of God," did not require any methodology to deal with the demons in a "simple and effective" way. Reid notes that the disciples in Acts of the Apostles, also dealt with spiritual evil power after they were baptized in the Holy Spirit and endued with power from on high (Luke 24:49; Acts 2:1 – 42).

Reid observes that the apostles used the Word of God as a weapon "to destroy the works of" evil and "establish the reality of the gospel in the hearts and minds of men." Reid summarized that "wherever the Apostles ministered, whether to Jew or Gentile," the Word of God was their weapon. In spiritual warfare, "The word of God is the means by which God makes Himself known, declares His will, and brings about His purposes." Reid explains that God's self-revelation "culminated in the sending of His Son, Jesus Christ, the incarnate Word of God empowered by the Spirit of God." Reid agrees with Robert Haldane that "the Gospel must be communicated to the minds of men through the external instrumentality of the Word, and by the internal agency of the Spirit."

Reid emphasizes "the role of the Holy Spirit in prayer" as another tool for spiritual warfare. Through prayer, the Holy Spirit came "to empower the Church." Reid holds that "The divine cooperation of the whole Trinity is at work in prayer: 'God the Holy Ghost writes our prayers, God the Son presents our prayers, and God the Father accepts our prayers.'" Reid reports Gordon D. Fee as seeing the role of the Holy Spirit in prayer as "our divine '*pray-er*,' the one through whom we pray, not the one to whom prayer is directed." Citing Romans 8:26, Reid confirms that the Spirit helps believers' infirmities concerning prayer, "for we know not what we should pray for as we ought" (Romans 8:26). Reid concludes, "There is no evidence in the New Testament to suggest that Christians are called to engage in an ongoing conflict with spiritual forces in the cosmic realm." Reid's project aligns with some of my views on baptism in the Holy Spirit, spiritual warfare, and the role of the Holy Spirit in prayer.

9

Theoretical Constructs of Baptism In The Holy Spirit

From the classical Pentecostal perspectives of the theoretical constructs for baptism in the Holy Spirit, Charles Fox Parham says that by receiving the baptism in the Holy Spirit, God seals a believer, and there is a guarantee that the believer will escape the tribulation of the last days with the assurance of rapture. He also says that the sealing of the believer takes place through the baptism in the Holy Spirit and not by a man or water baptism. Parham equates "the bride" with the 144,000 believers found in the book of Revelation 19:7. Parham believes that there is a need for verification when a person claims to be baptized in the Holy Spirit and that speaking in "a new foreign-understandable language (*xenolalia*)" is biblical evidence of Spirit baptism.

Ernest S. Williams disagrees with Parham's view of verification of whether a person is baptized in the Holy Spirit or not. E. Williams argues that every believer "possesses the Holy Spirit, but not every believer" is baptized in the Holy Spirit. In truth, the Holy Spirit also "dwells in all believers, yet not all believers know the full power of the Holy Spirit." Also, E. Williams says, "Baptism in the Holy Spirit differs from regeneration;" therefore, he argues that there is a difference between "having the Spirit" in regeneration and "being filled with the Spirit" in Spirit baptism. E. Williams agrees that regeneration cleanses one and prepares one for baptism in the Holy Spirit.

E. Williams continues, "In the new birth, the blood of Jesus cleanses and prepares" a believer ahead of baptism in the Holy Spirit, which is a definite experience. He believes that "the purpose of the baptism with [in] the Spirit" "is to be filled with spiritual power," as witnessed by the disciples in the upper room. The baptism in the Holy Spirit "does not consist of something" that people know only "by faith or mental assent," but by "the concreteness and definiteness" of the experience itself. E. Williams says that if one considers the believers' experience at Samaria (Acts 8:12), then baptism in the Holy Spirit follows regeneration.

Koo Dong Yun compares the Charismatic construct of Spirit baptism in Malines Document I with Larry Christenson's Lutheran construct, both of which reveal "the 'sacramental' context in which they construct their theologies of Spirit baptism." The Malines Document I explains "the meaning of baptism in the Spirit, the role of experience in a life of faith, and the function of the Charisma in the community." Yun presents Christenson as believing that there is only one baptism (Ephesians 4:5). Accordingly, "the rite of water baptism coincides with Spirit baptism when administered properly in faith." "In Christian initiation, one receives the Holy Spirit and becomes a Christian," and the Holy Spirit is given to each believer.

Donald L. Gelpi, from the Catholic perspective of the Spirit-baptism construct, explains baptism in the Holy Spirit as a whole "transformation process from initial faith to final, bodily resurrection." Gelpi developed "a triadic structure of experience" with "three relational variables: evaluations, decisions, and tendencies." He "construes Spirit baptism as an ongoing process of transformation." Gelpi says that "this process encompasses 'repentance, hope, faith, love, sanctification, and mutual service in response to the charismatic anointing of the Holy Spirit.'" He concludes that "baptism in the Holy Spirit is a lifetime process" and that "Spirit baptism cannot be reduced to a particular moment of graced experience."

*Karl Barth's Construct of Baptism in the Holy Spirit

Karl Barth developed his "Christocentric" construct from

Wilhelm Hermann's "Christocentrism," who "rejected philosophy and speculative theology." Barth's "Christocentrism" is "based on biblical exegesis" and on making Jesus Christ "the center of his theology." As part of Barth's contribution to the twenty-first-century theology, he "restored the doctrine of the Trinity as the central doctrine of the Church" through his Church Dogmatics. He distinguishes between baptism with the Holy Spirit and baptism with water. Barth believes that baptism with the Holy Spirit "signifies the divine subjective change which brings about human freedom." In contrast, baptism with water "alludes to the first human response to the divine change."

Initially, Barth saw baptism "as a sacrament and a means of grace." Later, Barth rejected infant baptism. Finally, Barth accepted "water baptism as a purely human act" but "insisted that Christians should" also receive water baptism. Barth looks at baptism in the Holy Spirit from the viewpoint of "divine subjective change." Therefore, in Barth's construct, "the quintessential element of Spirit baptism consists in divine change." The manifestation of Jesus Christ to humanity through his historical birth, life, death, and resurrection was objective. Barth holds that the "subjective change of God which comes about 'in' a human constitutes the baptism in the Holy Spirit."

Barth holds that "this subjective change effected by God,

which enables a person to see the objective reality of revelation in Jesus Christ, is the baptism in the Holy Spirit." Therefore, "without receiving the baptism in the Holy Spirit, a human being is not free to serve God." Yun concludes that in a real-life situation, elements such as the Word of Jesus Christ, when preached directly to a person, will cause a divine change, which is the beginning of a new Christian life and baptism in the Holy Spirit.

*The Normative Pattern
of Baptism in the Holy Spirit

Ervin discusses the "normative pattern" of baptism in the Holy Spirit along with the same design of Pentecost. Ervin sees the book of Acts as the basis for the normative pattern of baptism in the Holy Spirit, not the Epistles. Ervin explains, "As the baptism of John placed the candidate in the medium of water, so the baptism of Jesus places the Christian in the Spirit," and Jesus Himself is "the administrator of this Spirit-baptism." Ervin believes that "the normative evidence of" the baptism in the Holy Spirit "is a charismatic manifestation of the Spirit's personality and power." Furthermore, it was not only on the day of Pentecost that the disciples were all filled with the Holy Spirit and began to speak in other tongues as the Spirit gave them utterance. Ervin also links the normative pattern of baptism in the Holy Spirit to the fruits and gifts of the Holy Spirit. He says that Spirit baptism "is not per se an emotional experience, nor can the continuing fulness of the Spirit be equated with a transitory emotional experience." Ervin holds that "The manifestations of the charismata are the evidence of the Spirit's power."

Ervin cites the Apostle Paul's Pentecost as an example. Ervin explains that Paul's conversion or new birth occurred in a Pentecostal way, and Paul also was baptized in the Holy Spirit after his conversion (Acts 9:7). Ervin tells how Cornelius and his family received the baptism in the Holy Spirit after the Apostle Peter preached in his house. Therefore, Ervin concludes that "tongues are normative evidence of the baptism in the Holy Spirit in this place." Additionally, the Jewish believers who accompanied Peter knew that the Gentile converts had received the gift of baptism in the Holy Spirit because they heard them speaking in tongues and extolling God.

The Definition Of Baptism In The Holy Spirit

French L. Arrington holds that the books of Luke and Acts are the two original books of the Bible that support the doctrine of baptism in the Holy Spirit. Arrington defines the baptism in the Holy Spirit as a distinct and empowering experience for mission and worship after conversion. He says that Jesus is the agent for baptism in the Holy Spirit, the Spirit is the element, and the believers and followers of Jesus are the candidates who are immersed or baptized in the Spirit. Arrington notes that the term "baptism" means immersed. He says that John the Baptist immersed people into water baptism at the Jordan River. Jesus immerses believers into the Holy Spirit, empowering them for mission and service.

Randy Clark cites John Piper as saying that "being baptized with the Holy Spirit is when a person, who is already a believer, receives an extraordinary spiritual power for Christ-exalting ministry." Piper believes that being filled through Spirit baptism can bring "extraordinary power in ministry." Also, Frank Macchia concludes that "Spirit baptism is a baptism into the love of God that sanctifies, renews, and empowers until Spirit baptism turns all of creation into the final dwelling of God." Clark reports Henry I. Lederle's belief that "[Macchia] sees *glossolalia* as a symbol of empowered ministry that bridges linguistic and cultural boundaries."

Don Basham also believes that extraordinary power is associated with baptism in the Holy Spirit. Basham defines "baptism in the Holy Spirit" as "a second encounter with God (the first is conversion) in which the Christian begins to receive the supernatural power of the Holy Spirit into his life" (Acts 1:8). Basham states, "the second experience of God's power, the baptism in the Holy Spirit," is given to equip "the Christian with God's power for service. Clark believes that believers today can receive spiritual empowerment for the work they are called to do. He said subsequent to conversion, the people received a special endowment of power, inspiring witnessing and godly living. Clark concludes that baptism in the Holy Spirit is another spiritual blessing to be received following one's conversion experience. *The Apostolic Faith* newspaper reports, "The Baptism with the Holy Ghost is a gift of power upon the sanctified life; so, when we get it, we have the same evidence as the disciples received on the Day of Pentecost in speaking in new tongues." The paper declares that "The baptism with the Holy Ghost makes you a witness unto the uttermost parts of the earth. It gives you the power to speak in the languages of the nations."

Torrey explains that there are several phrases used in the Bible to denote baptism in the Holy Spirit. For example: "gift of the Holy Ghost," "the Holy Spirit fell on them," and "received the Holy Ghost." He says that baptism in the Holy Spirit is a definite experience so that one may know whether one "has received it or not." Additionally, Spirit baptism is a work of the Holy Spirit that is "separate and distinct from His regenerating work." Torrey sees regeneration and baptism in the Holy Spirit as not the same. He holds that a believer may be regenerated yet not baptized in the Holy Spirit. Torrey claims that after regeneration is the "second blessing" experience, which is the baptism in the Holy Spirit, and it can be received immediately. Torrey defines baptism in the Holy Spirit as "the Spirit of God coming upon the believer, taking possession of his faculties, imparting to him gifts not naturally his own, but which qualify him for the service to which God called him."

The view of *Tertullian* (ca. 155-240) is similar to that of Torrey, that baptism in the Holy Spirit "was not only about coming to Christ and repenting; it was also about Christ coming to the newly baptized in the filling of the Spirit, with the laying on of hands." St. John Chrysostom (AD 347-407) also believed that Spirit baptism occurs after regeneration. He speaks of being "baptized into the faith of Christ and being made worthy of the gift of the Spirit, given by the imposition of hands." Hart says, "Spirit baptism has frequently been at the center of controversy." Hart explains that "the sacramental traditions associate Spirit baptism with the sacrament of baptism itself." Through the lens of the Pentecostals and Charismatics, Hart declares that baptism in the Holy Spirit "is an empowerment for mission and ministry and is essential to the completion of the task."

In conclusion, we can observe the challenges that scholars face in attempting to define baptism in the Holy Spirit. My simple definition is that the baptism in the Holy Spirit is an unmerited Spirit-empowerment poured into an empty vessel-person from God for God's assignment on earth.

The Need For Baptism In The Holy Spirit

For believers to be like the Master, there is a need for baptism in the Holy Spirit. Why should believers need to be like the Master? A. B. Simpson said, "Both the One who makes men holy and those who are made holy are of the same family" (Hebrew 2:11). Jesus, the Master Himself, was born of the Spirit and was baptized in the Holy Spirit. He lived His life in the Spirit and produced His ministry through the empowerment of the Holy Spirit. In the New Testament, Jesus received the Spirit from His Father. In the same pattern, Jesus breathed upon his disciples, saying, *"Receive the Holy Spirit"* (John 20:22). Simpson believes that the coming of the Holy Spirit upon Jesus purposely was to connect him with power from on high. Jesus presumed that without this power, the disciples would not be able to function effectively in witnessing the Gospel globally (Acts 1:8). Jesus' breathing upon the disciples was "meant to connect it with Himself" in preparation for the outpouring of the Holy Spirit on the day of Pentecost. Simpson holds that the need for connecting with the Holy Spirit is evidence of the baptism in the Holy Spirit and shows that believers have been baptized unto death and raised into life; thus, they receive the Spirit from on high. Also, this is to make each person "a living being as real as Jesus Christ of Nazareth, and as real as our personality."

131

In conclusion, there is a need for baptism in the Holy Spirit in order to become Christ-like. Also, to be Christ-like is to be filled with the Holy Spirit like Jesus (Isaiah 42:1, 61). Jesus himself said:

"The Spirit of the Lord God is upon Me because the Lord has anointed Me to proclaim good news to the poor" – **Luke 4:18** (Isaiah 61:1).

Thus, in order to manifest the fruit of the Spirit and the gifts of the Spirit, Apostle Paul made it clear believers need the baptism in the Holy Spirit (Galatians 5:22 – 23; 1 Corinthians 12:1 – 11).

10

The Purpose of Baptism In The Holy Spirit

Peter Hocken "addressed the question of the relationship of Jesus Christ and the Holy Spirit in the event of baptism in the Spirit." He says that the purpose of baptism in the Holy Spirit is classically stated as the "enduement of power for ministry and service evidenced by the sign of speaking in tongues." Hocken cites Stanley Frodsham as saying, "The Pentecostal Baptism of the Holy Spirit brings a deeper and clearer revelation of our Lord and Savior Jesus Christ." For Hocken, "the meaning of Pentecost" is "the initial realization of God's plan to have a people who would be His very own, glorify Him, and declare His majesty" (Joel 2:28; Acts 2:27).

In his contribution, Grant Wacker expresses the views of

Higher Life and the non-Reformed Wesleyan holiness movements. Wacker reports that the Higher Life adherents insist that the primary purpose of baptism in the Holy Spirit "was to empower believers to serve the Church and witness for Christ." The non-Reformed Wesleyan holiness writers say that the main purpose of baptism in the Holy Spirit "was to eradicate 'inbred sin' and thereby break the stranglehold of selfish desires." Christopher Palmer also holds that the purpose of baptism in the Holy Spirit is empowerment for witnessing and as an indication of "Jesus' understanding of the role of the Spirit-power to witness."

Hart cites the Apostle Paul while discussing "the purifying dimension of the work of the Holy Spirit," and Hart sees the purpose of Spirit baptism as means by which believers are enabled and empowered to live holy lives. Hart believes, "Spirit baptism affects not only new birth and empowered witnessing; it also enables a continually transformed lifestyle." Billy Graham, Myles Munroe, and Andreas J. Köstenberger also share their views on the purpose of baptism in the Holy Spirit. For example, Graham held that "there is only one baptism with the Holy Spirit in the life of every believer," which "takes place at the moment of conversion," and it "was initiated at Pentecost;" thus, this baptism is regeneration. Graham believed that baptism in the Holy Spirit "is a collective operation of the Spirit of God," and that "it includes every believer." He says that "the purpose of the baptism with the Holy Spirit is to bring the new Christian into the body of Christ."

Munroe believed that the purpose of baptism in the Holy Spirit is to prepare believers "for our restored dominion assignment to make the earth into a replica of heaven." Munroe held that baptism in the Holy Spirit helps believers "yield" to the King, "allowing him to release in power what is already inside us." This baptism in the Holy Spirit is "like a forceful river; it is like waterpower harnessed as energy to run equipment, such as in a mill, for the betterment of humanity and its need." Köstenberger, attempting to explain what it means to be filled with the Spirit, says that in the Old Testament, the Spirit was given to enable "God's chosen person to carry out the commission given to him or her." He explains that the terminology "be filled with the Spirit" was mentioned only in Ephesians 5:18, and it was used in a "reference to being 'drunk with wine' (cf. also Luke 1:15; cf. Acts 2:4 and 2:13)." Therefore, the phrase "being filled with the Spirit' should be understood in a metaphorical sense of someone's being 'full' of a given substance (wine) or the spiritual (the Holy Spirit)."

Köstenberger relates that Paul prayed for "believers to be 'filled unto all the fullness of God,'" filled with "righteousness," "filled with the knowledge of God's will in all wisdom and spiritual understanding" (Ephesians 3:19; Philippians 1:11; Colossians 1:9; cf. 2:9-10;

Romans 15:13 – 14). Köstenberger cites the examples of individuals like Peter, Stephen, and Paul who were "filled with the Spirit" and empowered to witness the gospel. Köstenberger concludes that this infilling is to enable believers "for preaching, martyrdom or spiritual warfare." In Luke's narrative, he stated that "the entire community is filled with the Spirit" purposely to proclaim the gospel (Acts 4:31).

I agree with Köstenberger's view that believers need to seek the baptism in the Holy Spirit in order to fight against the unseen wicked spirits in heavenly places and to overcome the battle between the flesh and the spirit (Romans 7:15). Furthermore, believers cannot live holy lives, enjoy spiritual gifts, understand God's Word, fight spiritually, preach, pray, praise, and witness the gospel globally, without Spirit-empowerment, which is baptism in the Holy Spirit.

How To Receive
The Baptism In The Holy Spirit

Paul asked the disciples he met at Ephesus, "Did you receive the Holy Spirit when you believed?" (Acts 19:1). This question is relevant to today's Church. It is important to receive baptism in the Holy Spirit; thus, Jesus, the Spirit-baptizer, said that those who desire to be baptized in the Holy Spirit should ask for it. Jesus said, "If you then, though are evil, know how to give good gifts to your children, how much more will your Father in heaven give the Holy Spirit to those who ask him!" (Luke 11:13).

Also, after the initial baptism in the Holy Spirit, the Apostle Peter told his listeners, "Repent and be baptized, every one of you, in the name of Jesus Christ for the forgiveness of your sins. And you will receive the gift of the Holy Spirit" (Acts 2:38). To be baptized in the Holy Spirit, the Apostle Peter called for repentance and baptism for the remission of sins, in the name of Jesus.

Another Pentecostal practitioner, Kenneth Hagin, says that the gift of Holy Spirit baptism has already been given to believers for them to receive. Hagin places honoring and acting on God's Word as vital requirements for believers to receive the baptism in the Holy Spirit (Luke 11:11 – 13). Hagin explains that for the individuals who desire to be baptized in the Holy Spirit, they must have first received salvation in Christ. Also, he mentions that through the laying on of hands, a believer could be baptized in the Holy Spirit. Hagin concludes that after these requirements, a believer could be baptized in the Holy Spirit and begin to speak with new tongues (Acts 2:4, 10:46, 19:6; 1 Corinthians 14:2 – 15, 18, 27).

In line with both Hagin and the Apostle Peter, Torrey believes that people need to repent, confess their sins, receive salvation, and ask God in order to receive baptism in the Holy Spirit. Torrey explains that repentance is to have a change of mind "about God," "about Christ," and to renounce their sins. Torrey holds that there is a need for sinners and believers to confess their sins openly and to surrender to Jesus in order to receive baptism in the Holy Spirit. To desire baptism in the Holy Spirit by any believer, Torrey believes that water baptism should precede Spirit baptism (Acts 10:47). Torrey mentions other requirements for those seeking baptism in the Holy Spirit. They must be obedient to God, which means "total surrender to the will of God," because disobedience will hinder them from receiving the baptism in the Holy Spirit (Acts 5:38). Also, there is a need for the believer to thirst for the baptism in the Holy Spirit. Believers are expected to "thirst" and "desire" for Spirit baptism, but the desire must also be "pure" and not "selfish." Torrey believes that believers need to ask God to baptize them in the Holy Spirit (Luke 11:13).

In his conclusion, Torrey says that when believers ask God through prayer to baptize them with the Holy Spirit, they should believe that He will answer and give the gift to them. Torrey encourages believers that they should have faith and never doubt after they ask (Mark 11:24). Torrey asserts, "Every manifestation of the Baptism with the Holy Spirit in the New Testament was in new power in service."

The Sign Of Baptism In The Holy Spirit: Speaking In Tongues

The question about speaking in tongues as the initial evidence of the baptism in the Holy Spirit has generated great discussions. Scholars have asked: Is speaking in tongues the initial evidence of the baptism in the Holy Spirit? Is speaking in tongues for everybody? Is speaking in tongues necessary? Why should I speak with tongues? What is the value of speaking in tongues? How may I receive the gift of speaking in tongues? After receiving the gift of speaking in tongues, what next? Scholars have attempted to answer some of these questions. Anthony Hoekema declares, "The baptism of the believers in the Holy Spirit is witnessed by the initial physical sign of speaking with tongues."

Donald S. Metz, in his historical analysis of Pentecostalism, says that speaking in tongues was emphasized as evidence of the believer's entrance into a state of spiritual power and fellowship. Metz also believes, like Hoekema, that the term "speaking in tongues" is the initial physical sign of baptism in the Holy Spirit and is connected with the Greek term glossolalia meaning "tongue" or "language." Metz cites several Scriptures where unusual utterances or speaking in tongues occurred in the Old Testament (e.g. 1 Samuel 10:10). Metz argues that the Old Testament writers give no support to speaking in an unknown utterance as an essential part of religious experience. In line with Metz,

Turner reports, "The phenomenon of 'tongues' is mentioned with certainty in only two books of the New Testament: Acts and 1 Corinthians."

Therefore, is speaking in tongues necessary? Metz answers that Chrysostom sees the miracle at Pentecost as the antithesis of the Tower of Babel or as a reversal. Chrysostom interprets sin as the issue that caused the confusion and speaking of different tongues at the Tower of Babel. Macchia writes that the tongues on the Day of Pentecost "were a sign of the release of the Jesus story that the God of Israel is now also revealed as the God of the nations." Furthermore, the tongues spoken were "a sign of a global movement of the Spirit" beyond the high cultural, religious, race, and national "barriers that separated peoples from each other and brought them together in praise and service." Macchia explains that this new "movement of the Spirit in witness to Christ signals a new language as the beginnings of new creation in history."

In his answer to why tongues are necessary, Dorries explains that tongues speech functioned in the New Testament era both as an initial sign of the Spirit's empowerment and as a gift of the worship utterance for both personal and corporate edification. What does speak in tongues signify? Neil Hudson reports that A. A. Boddy believes that "the gift of tongues was the sign of having received the Spirit."

Why should Christians speak in tongues? Gordon Lindsay and Freda Lindsay answer: speaking in tongues has been foretold in prophecies in the Old Testament (Isaiah 28:11, 12). The Lindsays say that speaking in tongues in the New Testament is a fulfillment of the Old Testament prophecy (1 Corinthians 14:21). Before the Great Commission, Christ emphasized that believers should speak in tongues (Mark 16:15 – 17). The Lindsays observe that every one of the 120 disciples who were filled with the Holy Spirit on the Day of Pentecost spoke in tongues (Acts 2:1 – 4). Additionally, the first Gentiles to be saved received baptism in the Holy Spirit and spoke in new tongues (Acts 10:4 – 5). Finally, one of the outstanding figures in the Early Church, the Apostle Paul, also spoke in new tongues. Ervin holds that "whether stated or implied, it is a fair conclusion from the Biblical evidence that tongues are the 'external and indubitable proof' of the baptism in or filling with the Holy Spirit."

In conclusion, "As men without God have done good works, so also men without the fullness of the Holy Spirit have done much good." I believe that tongues are necessary, because "The Lord would have us receive the full promise of the Father, allowing Him to use us in an even greater way for His glory."

11

The Results of Being Baptized in the Holy Spirit

The results of baptism in the Holy Spirit have significantly impacted the lives of individuals and the Church. Arrington writes that the baptism in the Holy Spirit has led to an increase in spiritual empowerment, and having received the experience, some people have served the Lord well. Arrington explains that this experience often comes with a profound sense of God's presence, consecration, love, and compassion, as well as greater spiritual vitality in life and ministry. The results of Spirit baptism indicate that the experience is a wonderful provision of God that adds significantly to Christian life and ministry. Arrington asserts that out of Spirit baptism flows life that is lived to its fullest in dynamic communion with God. This experience brings believers closer to God through an intense fellowship with the Trinity. However, the primary result of baptism in the Holy Spirit is the power to evangelize the world (Acts 1:8). Arrington says, "Both power (Dunamis) and witness (Martus) point to empowerment by the Spirit to share the gospel with the lost."

Arrington argues that the coming of the Spirit of God was mainly to enable the Church to carry out the great commission to the ends of the earth. The disciples were empowered by the Spirit to give a powerful witness to what Jesus Christ did through preaching and the Holy Spirit. God confirmed their words through great signs and wonders wherever they went (Acts 2:22).

Arrington posits that one of the most significant results or signs of baptism in the Holy Spirit is speaking in tongues. He believes that speaking in tongues may be devotional, providing a means by which a believer may praise and worship God. As a result of baptism in the Holy Spirit, believers are able to live and practice lives of holiness and Christlikeness. Arrington notes, "A review of Church history discloses that spiritual gifts have been manifested through Christians in all ages."

*Biblical Examples of Baptism in the Holy Spirit

In his contribution, W. A. Criswell believes that the term baptism in the Holy Spirit is so much used and abused, and it was not mentioned in Luke-Acts (Matthew 3:11). Criswell observes that people have built their theology around the baptism in the Holy Spirit, and they teach it as a second work of grace. He argues that atonement for sins and justification for souls comes before the baptism in the Holy Spirit on earth. The coming of the Spirit of the Lord on the Day of Pentecost is the ascension gift of the Lord to His church. Criswell recognizes Christ as the primary "source or agent" and the Holy Spirit "is the immediate agent." Criswell explains, "The Spirit does the actual baptizing, joining believers in Christ to His body, the Church (Acts 2:37 – 38)."

Luke records examples of those baptized in the Holy Spirit in Acts of the Apostles. He said during Peter's sermon at Cornelius' house, "While Peter was still speaking these words, the Holy Spirit came on all who heard the message. For they heard them speaking in tongues and praising God" (Acts 10:44, 46). In Cornelius' story, the Spirit continued as the agent who baptized and joined the people into the body of Christ. Philip went to Samaria, and after he had preached the gospel, several people were converted to the Lord. Also, in Jerusalem, when they heard about the mighty works that God did through Philip in Samaria, they sent Peter and John to pray for them. And because the Holy Spirit had not yet come on them, Peter and John placed their hands on them, and they received the Holy Spirit (Acts 8:15 – 17, 19). The Apostle Paul at Ephesus met some

Gentiles, and he explained to them the difference between water baptism and baptism in the Holy Spirit. After they believed, "they were baptized in the name of the Lord Jesus." And when Paul had laid his hands upon them, "the Holy Spirit came on them" (Acts 19:1 – 6).

G. R. Beasley-Murray reports that the practice of laying on of hands is a common phenomenon in the Old Testament. It is connected with "the offering sacrifice," "the consecration of Levites in the service of the Temple," and "the imparting of a blessing" (Leviticus 1:3; Numbers 8:10; Genesis 48:14). In the first two instances, the "laying on of hands" means "to lean," and "by leaning hands on a person or animal, a man 'poured' his personality into him or it, hence making him or it into a substitute."

The Spiritual Gifts And Baptism In The Holy Spirit

James F. Stitzinger observes that almost every religious circle had shown interest in the subject of spiritual gifts. While discussing spiritual gifts and baptism in the Spirit, he presents the two views that "all gifts are for today" and that "some gifts were temporary and some permanent." The latter position says that "apostleship, prophecy, wisdom, knowledge, faith, miracles, healing, tongues, and interpretation of tongues" are among the temporary gifts. Stitzinger holds that the miraculous gifts ended with the apostles. At the same time, though, Stitzinger believes, "The primary goal of all the gifts is building up the body of Christ." He posits, "Apostleship was a foundational gift for the New Testament Church," but it was temporary.

While addressing the positions of four different groups on spiritual gifts, Stitzinger reports the cessationist group's view that:

> The miraculous gifts ceased with, or very soon after, the ministry of the apostles to whom – and to whom only they were given. It understands that the miraculous and non-miraculous gifts appear in the same lists in Scripture because they all came from the same source – God's grace and the Spirit's power, yet it recognizes that different gifts are given by God for different purposes.

He says that terms like "charisma" or "charismatic" are associated with spiritual gifts, and "charisma" means "a free and undeserved gift, an unmerited grace-gift from God's grace." Stitzinger observes that "grace-gifts are distributions of the Spirit's power. Spiritual gifts are diverse, and distinct among individuals," and "they all contain a gracious provision, a spiritual ministry, and an effect or activity." Furthermore, Stitzinger affirms that "God has always engaged in enabling and empowering through His Spirit." He explains that "spiritual gifts are given by God through Christ and are produced in the person whom the Holy Spirit indwells and controls."

Stitzinger then defines "spiritual gifts" as *any ability and accompanying spiritual ministry and effect that God, through Christ, enables a believer to use, or motivates him to use, for His glory, in the body of Christ, through the energizing work of the Spirit.* Therefore, Stitzinger explains that it is possible for individual believers to be gifted by God differently in order to "bring them to light, at salvation or later, but these abilities are only gifts when used for edification in the Church." The use of these enabling gifts "differ among Churches according to the needs of the Church." Stitzinger holds that these are what he calls the "permanent gifts" (evangelist, pastors and teachers, assistance, administration, exhortation, giving, and showing mercy), which "are the product of divine enabling and are clearly non-miraculous." These non-miraculous gifts lack the "ability to give new revelation," and do not "authenticate the apostolic testimony;" rather, they "exist for the purpose of edifying the body of Christ."

Sanders, in his discussion about gift and gifts, explains that "the gift of the Spirit is for every member of the body of Christ without any discrimination." He explains further that spiritual gifts are most of the time special, and they are given to individuals. Sanders argues, though, that there are still individuals who are ignorant about spiritual gifts. Therefore, he emphasizes that spiritual gifts are not given to just a few or specific people. Sanders holds that every believer has the manifestation of gifts within them. Sanders' view is that not everyone who has gifts is exercising the gifts with which they have been endowed by God. Along the line of Stitzinger's thoughts, Sanders declares that the purpose for receiving spiritual gifts "is not for self-edification, neither is it for a special enduement of Spirit for a specific person, but for the profit and edification of the Body of Christ."

In conclusion, Sanders explains further that there are diversities of spiritual gifts and that no one gift is common to all Christians, and that it is not possible for one individual to possess all these gifts. Sanders disagrees with "those who contend that the miraculous gifts completely passed away, but it is difficult to maintain in the light of the Church and missionary history."

12

Practitioners And Practical Applications

Vinson Synan reports that according to researcher David Barrett, "As of 2006, the Pentecostal-Charismatic Renewal had appeared in three major phases." Accordingly, the Neo-Charismatic wave began in about 1980, and "individuals participating were first called the Post-denominational Charismatics and later the neo-Charismatics," and all three movements spread across Africa, Asia, and Latin America.

*Reinhard Bonnke

In Africa, Reinhard Bonnke, a German Pentecostal evangelist, became a representative of the Neo-charismatic movement. Bonnke's crusades brought "as many as one million conversions" to Christ "in a single service."

Bonnke, a pastor, attended Bible College in Wales. While a missionary, he founded the international ministry of Christ for all Nations (CfaN). In Lesotho, in Africa, "God placed upon his heart the vision of" the African continent with a mandate to reach Africa, "from Cape Town to Cairo and from Dakar to Djibouti" to proclaim the Gospel. He is known for holding meetings in a tent with thousands in attendance. In his over forty-five years of evangelistic ministry, he reached "more than 77 million documented decisions" of people who gave their lives to Christ. His ministry strategies include discipleship training, equipping Church leaders, and organizing "Fire Conferences." He developed the "Full Flame Film Series" of eight films "aimed at inspiring and challenging the Church to Holy Spirit evangelism."

In Bonnke's evangelistic crusades, he preached and taught more about the role of the Holy Spirit in evangelism, baptism in the Holy Spirit, speaking in tongues, spiritual gifts, and warfare. Bonnke believed that "the Holy Spirit is God in action on earth" and that "He is the power of Pentecost." The Spirit "is the Third Person of the Trinity" and is God "at work on earth." Furthermore, "everything that God does here, outside of heaven, is by His Spirit." Moreover, the Spirit "is the essence of the Christian faith, brought to us by the Gospel," and "there is no Christianity without Him." Bonnke also states that "The supreme work of the Spirit is salvation." Holy Spirit power cannot be generated by "prayer, time, effort, good works, or anything else" because "the Father gives us the Spirit as a gift."

Bonnke declares that "the Spirit is our empowering strength for witness" so that "all we are conveys the truth, not only by miracles but by a Spirit-filled life." Additionally, the Spirit of God, the Holy Spirit, is the divine power agency doing the work. Bonnke continues that the Holy Spirit is real, and this baptism means immersion in the Spirit. He likens the baptism in the Holy Spirit to the dedication of Solomon's temple, when "the glory of God came forth from the Holy of Holies." For Bonnke, this event was an outward manifestation showing "God has taken up his dwelling place" (John 14:23). He said, when the baptism of the Holy Spirit takes place, the Holy Spirit "fills not only the shrine of the believer's heart but their whole being." Bonnke holds that the baptism in the Holy Spirit is not merely an incoming power but God Himself, the Holy Spirit.

Bonnke states that believers can understand the doctrine of baptism in the Holy Spirit "through the resurrection of Jesus" (Acts 1:4 – 5, 8). Before the resurrection, Jesus already explained the nature of the Holy Spirit to His disciples, that the Spirit will be a counselor and will turn them into torches. Jesus told the disciples ahead that "Apart from me, you can do nothing" (John 15:5). On the Day of Pentecost, Jesus filled them with Himself, gave them utterances to speak in tongues, and they became a model for the Christians. Bonnke says that living life in the Spirit is the secret of the disciples. Bonnke believes that baptism in the Holy Spirit was for them as an individual, and not "for the whole Church."

Is baptism in the Holy Spirit a second blessing after being born again? In his view, Bonnke compares baptism in the Holy Spirit with atonement, for which there are various theories. Bonnke believes that Jesus does baptize in the Holy Spirit, and that believers do receive power when the Holy Spirit comes upon them, and that this is His work and that believers are His agents. Bonnke concludes, "We have no alternative to the power of the Spirit, no method, manner, scheme, or approach. The Spirit must do the work. The world still needs saving, still needs convincing, and it is impossible to do without the Holy Spirit." Bonnke says that Jesus admonished believers to ask, seek, and knock on the door by faith to be Spirit-filled. The baptism in the Holy Spirit is received by faith, "but the evidence is signs following."

Bonnke accepts speaking in tongues as the initial evidence of the baptism in the Holy Spirit. He holds that speaking in tongues is both biblical and theological, and it was standard practice in the early Church (1 Corinthians 14:18). In the New Testament, the Holy Spirit is always linked with ecstatic manifestations of the Spirit. At any point where this tangible evidence was absent, it was proof that people had not received the Spirit. Bonnke explains that people do not "learn how" to speak in tongues and that baptism in the Holy Spirit is not an "achievement." Also, it is neither a spiritual pose nor simply a denominational doctrine. God does this, and believers are passive recipients of this spontaneous grace. With constant preaching of the baptism in the Holy Spirit at Bonnke's crusades, many people have been saved. The fire of the Spirit has fallen, and this fire has ignited everything that it touches, and it has spread across continents.

In his crusades, Bonnke has observed that when the Spirit comes upon people unexpectedly, it is common to see many people shaking, falling, making meaningless cries, uttering animal noises, climbing trees, and bursting into unspeakable emotions, like drunkards. Bonnke calls the reactions of people being filled with the Spirit as "froth." Being baptized in the Spirit is dynamic and not a sacramental gesture by a priest. Bonnke holds that speaking in tongues involves surrendering to God physically, not just in the heart and that speaking in tongue is where the human and divine wills come together. He says that believers can only speak in tongues as the Spirit enables them (Acts 2:4). Bonnke declares that conversion or the new birth is evidence that people have received the divine nature. "Receiving the Spirit is the consummation of life and being filled with the Spirit was part of God's plan."

In conclusion, Bonnke mentions the importance of

spiritual gifts as "God-given means" by which "the timid soul can become bold, and the defensive person can become aggressive." The Holy Spirit's gifts "are far greater than anything that the occult can manufacture." The gifts of the Spirit are "effective", and "they are God's powerful weapons." Furthermore, "The gifts of the Spirit are not to be reserved for some future occasion but are to be used today."

*David O. Oyedepo

For decades, Bishop Oyedepo has been part of the Charismatic renaissance that has swept through the African Continent. Oyedepo is one of the principal leaders and practitioners of the Charismatic movement in Nigeria. Oyedepo is a pastor and author, as well as the founder and presiding Bishop of Living Faith Ministries International Worldwide (Winners Chapel) in Ota, Ogun State, Nigeria. Oyedepo was called into ministry with the specific mandate to liberate mankind from all forms of evil oppression. He established the Church on twelve ministry pillars: faith, Word, prayer, consecration, prosperity, vision, wisdom, success, signs and wonders, the Holy Spirit, and praise. Oyedepo's Church, with a 50,000-seat auditorium capacity, was built on 10,000 acres of land, and it "runs about four services every Sunday."

Oyedepo preaches more about the Holy Spirit and baptism in the Holy Spirit as an empowering tool for evangelism. He says that everyone needs the Holy Spirit to make a difference in the world. He holds that no one can make meaning or go places on earth as a Christian until one is endued with power from on high, which only the Holy Spirit gives. Oyedepo believes that "the unction of the Holy Spirit is what guarantees the motion of life." The Holy Spirit is not just tongues! "He is the gift of God for our dignity on the earth" and "the beauty of Zion." Oyedepo declares, "we need the power of the Holy Spirit to matter on planet earth."

Oyedepo preached more about the important role played by the Holy Spirit in the Church and among the believers. He says that the Holy Spirit brings news from heaven to help believers make news on earth, and He connects believers to the wisdom of heaven. The Spirit is the communicator of the secrets of God (1 Corinthians 2:10). The Holy Spirit gives guidance and destroys yokes (Isaiah 10:27). The Spirit is the power of God from above and is above every other power on the earth (Acts 1:8). The Holy Spirit is the power against unclean spirits. Oyedepo affirms that "the lifting of the Church is tied to the outpouring of the Spirit, and the lifting of the ministry, is tied to the outpouring of the Spirit upon our lives."

Furthermore, for believers to experience the baptism in the Holy Spirit requires repentance and righteousness. It is impossible for believers to encounter the outpouring of the Spirit until righteousness is fulfilled. Oyedepo explains that the "rain of righteousness prepares the ground for the rain of the Spirit" (Acts 3:19). When someone repents, is converted, and has sins blotted out, then that person begins to enjoy times of refreshing that come from the outpouring of the Spirit. Oyedepo notes that there is a difference between baptism in the Holy Spirit and the outpouring of the Spirit. For believers, "power" "is an essential tool for kingdom exploits and witnessing." Furthermore, Oyedepo declares that "the manifestations of the Holy Spirit in the last days is nothing but POWER." In spiritual warfare, the role of the Holy Spirit is to subdue the powers of the enemies and to make believers rule over their enemies, as well as to disarm all wickedness, subdue kingdoms, and bring about righteousness (Psalm 110:1-3; Hebrew 11:33; Isaiah 28:21-22).

Oyedepo emphasizes the subjects of power and baptism in the Holy Spirit. He claims that the endowment of power from above began with the baptism in the Holy Spirit. He posits that the proof of the Spirit's presence (speaking in tongues) is "proof that the powers of heaven are resident on your inside." Like the disciples in Acts of the Apostles, when the Spirit resides in believers, it is a proclamation that "we are power carriers in the kingdom" (Luke 10:19). Oyedepo suggests that anytime believers are faced with challenges, they should "speak in tongues to awaken their spiritual consciousness and bring Satan under judgment" (John 16:8-11). Oyedepo exclaims, "Power is the requirement for total release."

Oyedepo goes on to explain the types of power that are available for believers in Christ. There is a power that is connected to the new birth, which is the foundation of new life in Christ Jesus. The new birth is an initiation into the realm of power; it is also a spiritual initiation into the realm of the covenant (Luke 10:19). Also, the power of God can manifest at different levels. After a person becomes born again, that person operates from a spiritual dimension level, which is likened to a well of water (John 4:14). The water represents the Holy Spirit (John 7:38-39). At salvation, the Holy Spirit operates in believers at a well level. At baptism, it graduates to a river level. At the rain level, the Spirit begins to operate at the anointing level (Zechariah 10:1). Oyedepo describes regeneration as a new birth in Christ Jesus. In regeneration, a believer begins to live out of the ordinary by the power of God at work in the person (2 Corinthians 5:17).

In conclusion, Oyedepo says that those who are born of the Spirit belong to the extraordinary class of people who call divine forces into operation, like the wind. They blow and operate outside the ordinary; being born of the Spirit makes a person a spirit (John 3:5-6). Regeneration is much more than merely responding to an altar call: it is about having an in-depth understanding of a person's new status, which reflects the heavenly life. Oyedepo declares that the new status in Christ is the beginning of one's journey into a life of the miraculous (1 Peter 2:9).

*David Yonggi Cho

Young-hoon Lee discusses "the history, development, characteristics, and influence of [Cho's] Church in relation to" his ministry. D. Cho "was born on February 14, 1936, in Wooljoo County, Kyung-name Province, in the southern part of Korea, while the country was under Japanese occupation." D. Cho gave his life to Christ through a young Christian girl who gave him a Bible and told the Gospel to him. He began to study the biblical concept of divine healing sometime after he was healed. In 1958, D. Cho started a "tent Church," which went through a "pioneering period" from 1958 to 1961. During this time, D. Cho's Church led the Pentecostal faith in Korea through "its strong Full Gospel message and divine healing." Under D. Cho's leadership, between 1961 and 1973, Cho's Church grew, and it promulgated "the Pentecostal faith in the Korean Church" until finally, it became the leader of "the Holy Spirit movement of the entire Korean Church."

Lee, while discussing D. Cho's ministry, says that D. Cho's emphasis on baptism in the Holy Spirit with "subsequent signs such as speaking in tongues" and divine healing is part of "the driving forces" that have led to the development and success of the Church in South Korea. The congregation became transformed through D. Cho's powerful teachings, and they began to preach the Word of God to others. Lee reports that prayer became one of the most crucial parts in D. Cho's ministry.

D. Cho created powerful fasting and prayer opportunities and devoted himself to prayer day and night in the Church.

Lee explains that D. Cho's ministry strategies include effective training for the lay leaders, as well as developing a "cell-unit system" based on Exodus 18. Through the cell-unit system, D. Cho has been able to minister to more than 700,000 members. Lee notes, "The primary characteristic of this period was the work of the Holy Spirit experienced in the community," and it led to "revival and renewal of the Church as a community," which helped individuals experience baptism in the Holy Spirit. Like the Church in Acts of the Apostles, "The outpouring of the Spirit restored the Christian lives" in YFGC during this period. With this development, YFGC began to take the leadership "role in the Holy Spirit movement of the Korean Churches."

As an organization, YFGC conducts "seven worship services each Sunday, three services each Wednesday, and two each Saturday," and it has ten departments. The Church created a "Department of Pastoral and Theological Studies of the International Theological Institute" for training pastors and lay leaders. The Church's Mission Department supports world evangelism mission leaders of various mission groups. The Holy Spirit movement at YFGC has distinguishing elements, which include preaching about salvation, faith in the Word of God, experiencing the Holy Spirit, and world evangelization. Lee explains that "Cho's Bible-based sermons have contributed to the growth of YFGC," and "the expansion of the Holy Spirit movement."

Lee continues, "The framework of Cho's sermons" is based on "the five-fold gospel and three-fold blessing." The "five-fold gospel" includes: "the gospel of salvation; the gospel of the fullness of the Holy Spirit; the gospel of divine healing; the gospel of blessing; and the gospel of the second coming of Jesus Christ." Next, "The three-fold blessing is based on 3 John 2." Lee writes about D. Cho's emphasis that it is only through "the help of the Spirit" that these messages can be effective to "reach people and change them to trust in Jesus completely." Lee discussed the basic concepts of D. Cho's ministry as follows: "Cho is a man of prayer," and he believes that "prayer is hard and is a long process." D. Cho's traditional Pentecostal view believes that "baptism in the Holy Spirit is an experience distinct from conversion."

According to Lee, different denominations reject D. Cho's position on baptism in the Holy Spirit. D. Cho sees baptism in the Holy Spirit as "a second blessing after conversion," but John Wesley describes "second blessing" as "sanctification or as the wholeness of Christ." "Charles G. Finney, Dwight L. Moody, Reuben A. Torrey, and J. W. Chapman" are of the same view as Wesley; therefore, "The doctrine of Spirit-baptism is an integral part of the Holy Spirit movement." Lee says that D. Cho remains resolute on the issue of external signs in relation to Spirit baptism. D. Cho argues that speaking in tongues is a sign of Spirit-baptism and that it "is the most common and unique external sign." D. Cho classifies speaking in tongues "into two categories: 'sign' and 'gift.'" Accordingly, the members of YFGC are encouraged to be baptized in the Holy Spirit, speak to "edify the Church," become "witnesses to Christ," and be "armed with the power of the Holy Spirit."

In summary, Lee believes that the Holy Spirit movement of YFGC has contributed to D. Cho's ministry. YFGC's Holy Spirit movement has promoted "the Personhood of the Holy Spirit," and the Korean Churches have become more interested in the Holy Spirit as the third person of the Trinity. Until D. Cho's work, many Korean Churches were "almost ignorant of and uninterested in the ministry of and fellowship with the Holy Spirit." Today in Korea, many Christians have gained knowledge through D. Cho's teaching on how they could "minister and work with the Holy Spirit." It has been observed that D. Cho often says, "Holy Spirit, we acknowledge, welcome, and trust you."

Simon K. H. Chan looks at D. Cho's pneumatology, and Chan says that "the doctrine of the Holy Spirit has played a very vital role in his understanding of the Christian life and mission." Chan reports that D. Cho often refers to the Holy Spirit in his writings; however, "his theology of the Spirit is largely implicit rather than explicit." Chan highlights some of the features of D. Cho's "teachings concerning the Holy Spirit" and critiques "certain pneumatological motifs."

According to Chan, D. Cho's teachings on the Holy Spirit are based on "the classical Pentecostal position." D. Cho "believes in speaking in tongues as the 'initial evidence' of baptism in the Holy Spirit and that it is an experience distinct from the new birth." D. Cho "sees the Christian life as progressing towards a deeper faith" with the infilling of the Holy Spirit. Chan reports that D. Cho "insists that every cell leader must be 'filled with the Spirit.'" Chan describes D. Cho "as an 'unreconstructed' Pentecostal" concerning his doctrinal stance on baptism in the Holy Spirit. D. Cho's teachings and "Bible Study for New Christians" are grounded in Christian traditional beliefs that are shared by Christians globally. Chan reviews some of D. Cho's theological issues. He "is more concerned with implementing what he believes to be true rather than reflecting on the truth and drawing out its larger ramifications." Chan reports that "Cho refers to the Holy Spirit as the one who spans the ages by making present the great events of the past." Chan characterizes "Cho's pneumatology as a practical pneumatology."

Chan says that D. Cho "considers the Holy Spirit as the 'senior partner' in God's business of winning souls." Chan questions the scriptural basis for D. Cho's prayer verbiage.

Chan believes that D. Cho thinks "of the triune God as simply three coordinates with whom we sustain an intimate relationship," so that just as believers pray to the Father and the Son, D. Cho holds that we should separately "pray to the Spirit." Chan agrees that Christians "need to recognize the Holy Spirit as a person," but that this should be done by recognizing "his distinctive role in the triune relationship." Chan explains that the Scripture clearly shows that believers should direct their prayers "to God the Father and to the Son," but "there is no instance of prayer directed to the Spirit." Referencing Yves Congar's magisterial study, Chan states that "the Holy Spirit is always the one who points us to the Father and the Son. The Spirit is the person 'without a personal face.' The Spirit's role as the third person in the divine economy of salvation is not to draw attention to Himself but to point us to the Son. The Spirit is glorified precisely when Christ is glorified."

Chan notes that "when Cho refers to speaking in tongues as speaking the language of the Spirit, he sees it as the language of personal communication and intimacy with the Holy Spirit." Chan disagrees because he believes that the intimacy is with the Father. "It is the Spirit who creates the intimacy between the believers and God the Father" "to whom we speak by the indwelling Spirit" (Romans 8:26), and it is the Spirit "who dwells within us to enable us to address God as 'Abba, Father' (Romans 8:15)." Chan declares that except believers understand the appropriate Scripture-based "distinctive role of the Spirit in relation to the Father and the Son, there is a danger of giving the Spirit an independent status and divorce the work of the Spirit from the Father and the Son."

Chan sees problems with D. Cho's "five-fold gospel with a three-fold blessing," which "is a central motif" throughout his preaching. Chan believes that the concept is theologically weak, and the "problem with the three-fold blessing is that it is set within an inadequate conception of salvation-history. This misconception" is "due to a failure to understand the proper role of the Holy Spirit in the economy of salvation." Chan questions, "what sort of pneumatology is implied in Cho's attempt to maintain the 365-day-a-year revival?" Chan explains that "the main weakness in Cho's pneumatology lies at the point where he introduces his own teachings into the 'full gospel,' namely, the 'blessing' in the five-fold gospel." Chan submits:

> When pneumatology hangs loose from the doctrine of the Trinity, the Spirit begins to take a life of His own instead of being seen in relation to the triune economy of salvation. The Spirit is God's distinctive gift to the Church between the ascension and the parousia. This is the period of redemptive history characterized by what Farrow calls "the ascension or parousia differential" in which the Spirit takes the place of the absent Christ.

Nevertheless, from D. Cho's personal perspective, he says, "God's divine executive agent in the world today is the Holy Spirit. His work is powerful and continues steadily in the lives of Christians who have sought His help. The Holy Spirit can never be underestimated." D. Cho believes, "The measure of our faith is in direct proportion to our communion with the Holy Spirit. That through the communion of the Holy Spirit, we receive spiritual blessings, and we tell Him our earnest desires." D. Cho explains that "communion" means "fellowship," and "Without fellowship with the Holy Spirit, there can be no spiritual life, no faith with power and victory." D. Cho holds that the coming of the Holy Spirit into the world is to work "in partnership with believers, to quicken dead spirits by witnessing the grace of Jesus Christ" (John 15:26, 27). D. Cho notes that "the Holy Spirit, whom Jesus sent," also came "in the midst of fire" (Acts 2:2-3).

D. Cho compares the Spirit with some of the characteristics of fire. He says that "fire burns away that which is unwanted" and "fire provides us with light, which enlarges the sphere and hours of our activity." Like fire, "the Holy Spirit provides us with the power of heaven, urgently needed for our personal lives of faith and for the ministry of gospel preaching." D. Cho believes, "It is reckless to start the work of the gospel without receiving the divine power provided by the fire of the Holy Spirit."

D. Cho argues that "regeneration always comes first"

before baptism in the Holy Spirit. The Holy Spirit always goes a step beyond regeneration, and this is what baptism in the Holy Spirit is all about. D. Cho explains "the difference between regeneration and baptism in the Holy Spirit."

Citing examples and patterns of baptism in the Holy Spirit among believers and Gentiles in the Acts of Apostles, D. Cho says:

> Regeneration is the experience of receiving the life of the Lord by being grafted into the body of Christ through the Holy Spirit and the Scriptures. The baptism in the Holy Spirit is the experience in which Jesus fills believers with the power of God for ministry, service, and victorious living. Regeneration grants a person everlasting life, while baptism in the Holy Spirit grants regenerate believers the power of God to preach Christ.

In conclusion, D. Cho proclaims that "without the baptism of the Holy Spirit, the Church today" can never display God's power like the early Church – "a combative, challenging," and victorious power to evangelize a generation. Based on the assumptions that today's Christians are "powerless" and lack the fullness of the Holy Spirit, D. Cho declares that "we should pray to receive the fullness of the Holy Spirit," which is the "tremendous power of God for service." Thus, if a Christian is to have power and authority "to carry out the ministry and service of God," then he or she "must have baptism in the Holy Spirit."

*Oral Roberts

Daniel D. Isgrigg discusses how the baptism in the Holy Spirit has shaped the ministry of Roberts. Isgrigg looks at the significance of baptism in the Holy Spirit in Roberts' early life, as well as his ministry and work. Isgrigg says that Roberts, the founder of Oral Roberts University, was "one of the most important religious figures" and evangelists "in the twentieth century." Roberts became well-known in the 1950s through "his large-scale tent crusades," "television programs," powerful divine healing services, and his teachings on baptism in the Holy Spirit and Spirit-empowerment. Isgrigg reports that Robert's ministry has had a "profound influence on the Spirit–empowered movement," as his "ministry focused on salvation, sanctification, and the baptism in the Spirit," in addition to healing.

Roberts grew up in a poor Pentecostal home with his parents who, after "they were saved, sanctified, and filled with the Holy Spirit," became "Pentecostal Holiness pastors and evangelists." Roberts was impacted by his parent's preaching at revivals, but he ran from God and his parents, returning because he had tuberculosis. One night at his sickbed, at the point of death in July 1935, Roberts surrendered his life to Jesus. At 17, after the ceaseless prayers of his father, Roberts received his miraculous healing from tuberculosis. He was anointed by George Moncey, who "rebuked the tuberculosis," and Roberts "felt the power of God touch" him. Later, at a Pentecostal Holiness meeting, Roberts was baptized in the Holy Spirit with evidence of speaking in tongues.

Isgrigg reports that Roberts "received his license as a Pentecostal Holiness minister" when he was eighteen, and for three years, he was an evangelist. After this, Roberts became a pastor in Fuquay Spring, North Carolina, then in Shawnee, Oklahoma, at the Pentecostal Holiness Church. While there, "Roberts became a regular contributor to the denominational paper, The Pentecostal Holiness Advocate." In writing for the East Oklahoma Conference News, "he proclaimed, 'The greatest need of the hour for the conference is to have a revival break out in every Church.'"

While in college in Enid, Oklahoma, God spoke to Roberts saying, "Son, don't be like other men. Don't be like any denomination. Be like Jesus and heal like He did." After this, Roberts read through the Gospels and Acts to find out the secret behind the healing power of Jesus Christ, and he came to understand that it was the Holy Spirit. Roberts learned that baptism in the Holy Spirit "was not a denominational distinctive or even an important religious experience;' rather, it "was a divine command from God." Furthermore, "having the baptism in the Holy Spirit was the same as 'having Jesus Christ in his flesh by my side.'"

According to Isgrigg, Roberts "developed a methodology for his healing ministry grounded in the reality of the living presence of Jesus through the Holy Spirit." During tent meetings, crusades, and television programs, Roberts waited for the move of the Holy Spirit before he went to the pulpit to preach. As Roberts' tent meetings grew, so did the number of seekers of baptism in the Holy Spirit increase. Roberts began "to see himself not only as a healing evangelist but also as a Holy Spirit evangelist who would bring a new generation into the baptism in the Holy Spirit."

Isgrigg also discusses Roberts' views concerning the Holy Spirit, baptism in the Holy Spirit, speaking in tongues, and salvation. Citing the Apostle Paul, Roberts believed that speaking in tongues should be a frequent event that "was intended to be a 'normal experience' as part of one's relationship with God." As initial evidence of Spirit baptism, the concept of speaking in tongues was considered "the 'release of the Spirit.'" Roberts believes that speaking in tongues "is more than an evidence, more than a sign, more than for personal release in edification; it is also a power release." Isgrigg reports that Roberts adopted the habit of praying in the Spirit as part of his ministry strategy

169

and that this had a great impact on his healing ministry. Roberts holds, "The benefit of speaking in tongues, then, is that every time one prays, they release edification and power."

However, whether the baptism in the Holy Spirit comes before the language of the Spirit – speaking in tongues, Roberts says:

> The baptism in the Holy Spirit comes first because the infilling of the Holy Spirit is what causes and enables us to speak with the prayer language of the Spirit. The "speaking in tongues" doesn't cause the baptism in the Spirit to take place, but it is the indwelling of the Holy Spirit in your spirit that gives you the instant ability to speak to God in tongues, which is a true communication of your spirit with Him (Acts 2:4-5). THE REAL PURPOSE OF THE PRAYER LANGUAGE OF THE SPIRIT IS TO HELP OUR INTELLECT AND OUR UNDERSTANDING. For he that speaketh in an unknown tongue speaketh not unto men, but unto God (1 Corinthians 14:2).

Roberts presents his own perspective on various subjects, as discussed above. Roberts believes that "charisma" is "God believing in the human being and imparting to him a gift of the Holy Spirit," which is "a gift given by the grace of God — unmerited favor." With regards to the first coming of the Holy Spirit, Roberts believes that "the purpose of the Paraclete, the Holy Spirit, was to bring back the unlimited greater Christ" to believers in the power of the Spirit. Roberts explains that after the ascension, the Holy Spirit became Jesus' "personal representative" on earth. For example, Roberts holds that the essence of God's visitation to the Gentiles through Peter and the Holy Spirit is part of God's plan for the world.

Reading the events that happened to Peter before being sent to Cornelius' house at Joppa gave Roberts impetus to study more about the doctrine of baptism in the Holy Spirit. From this, Roberts believes, "The whole purpose of baptism in the Holy Spirit is to cause Jesus, who is Love, to EXPLODE in our hearts, with power from on high, to fill our inner man until it's like rivers of living water rolling up." In reply to his wife, Evelyn's question on publicly announcing Spirit baptism, Roberts replies that there is no need for publicity when a person is baptized in the Holy Spirit. It is a "very personal" experience, and it should "come out of you in love, in a deeper prayer life."

Roberts declares, "The keynote of the baptism in the Holy Spirit" is power. This is "the power of enablement," which "is present to some degree in both conversion and sanctification. Its fullness is received after the baptism with the Holy Ghost has become an integral part of one's life, and one continues to walk in the Spirit." Roberts explains that this enabling power will enable "one to become like Jesus" after receiving the baptism in the Holy

Spirit. This is an explosive power to witness about the person of Jesus Christ and the power to become witnesses wherever Christians find themselves. Roberts notes that the disciples received the enabling power on the Day of Pentecost, and even after Jesus' ascension, this power still abides and links them daily to Jesus to make believers His true witnesses. Roberts explains that, like the first disciples, believers today are faced with the same challenges; nevertheless, Jesus has given to all believers the same assignment.

Additionally, Roberts says, "The enabling power that will make us explosive witnesses of Christ" is the "same power that is inherent in the baptism with the Holy Ghost." Therefore, "entering into this power is as imperative for us as it was for" the first disciples. However, "receiving the Holy Ghost in His fullness does not mean that one will automatically use the power to become a witness of Jesus Christ." Roberts writes, though, "Power has always characterized the ministry of Christ and Christianity." Roberts concludes that Christians have power "to deliver people from sin, disease, demons, and fear" (Matthew 28:18). Roberts teaches that during the early years of Christianity, "The needs of the people were met 'through the power and demonstration of the Spirit'" (Acts 2). According to the Apostle Paul, the gospel is "the power of God because it is inbreathed by the Holy Ghost" (Romans 1:16). Also, men were inspired by the Holy Spirit to write the Bible, and whenever "those Spirit-anointed words were spoken by a Spirit-baptized witness, the words became 'the power of God.'"

Roberts argues further, "This power of the Holy Ghost is more explosive than the power experienced in salvation." In Acts 1:8, the word "power" "denotes dynamite, explosive power, the power of enablement." Roberts declares that "since that same power is available to all believers today, it is also true that we can fellowship and experience the presence of Jesus Christ" in our midst.

Roberts believes, "Being filled with the Holy Ghost provides power, enabling us to reflect and reproduce Jesus Christ in our generation so that He meets the needs of people in our day." According to Roberts, "Jesus teaches us that as the Holy Spirit directs our lives, we will have explosive power to share Him with the people throughout the world." Roberts says, "This baptism provides an inner power that becomes an outward force to bring the reality of Christ to others. To help release this power, the Holy Ghost gives the believer a new tongue." Roberts holds that in order for believers to be baptized in the Holy Spirit, they need to take themselves "out of the realm of fear," "resistance to receiving must be overcome," and they "must study" the Word of God. Believers should "be willing to bypass [their] intellect" through prayer, and "the Holy Spirit will flow forth as a river."

Roberts concludes that "The baptism with the Holy

Spirit is a tremendous experience. It is the descent of God in greater fullness into man and the ascent of man more completely into God. It is God, and total man blended in oneness. It is really a miracle."

13

Reflections On Baptism In The Holy Spirit

Baptism in the Holy Spirit remains one of the most important foundations of Pentecostal Churches today. Everything about baptism in the Holy Spirit started on the Day of Pentecost and continued into the twenty-first-century contemporary Church. Luke records in his Gospel that John the Baptist answered those who came to the Jordan River for water baptism by saying:

"I baptize you with water. But one who is more powerful than I will come, the thongs of whose sandals I am not worthy to untie. He will baptize you with the Holy Spirit and fire" – **Luke 3:16**.

Luke also mentions that Jesus, before His ascension,

promised the disciples that they would be baptized in the Holy Spirit. Luke records Jesus as saying:

"For John baptized with water, but in a few days you will be baptized with the Holy Spirit" – **Acts 1:5**.

During water baptism at the Jordan River, John the Baptist gave a powerful testimony of how Jesus Himself was baptized in the Holy Spirit before the beginning of His earthly ministry. John now testifies of Jesus, declaring that he really did not know that Jesus was the one until John saw the Spirit of God descending and remaining upon Him. The one who sent John to baptize told him that the one upon whom he saw the Spirit descend and remain was the one that would baptize with the Holy Spirit. John the Baptist said:

"I would not have known him, except the one who sent me to baptize with water told me, The man on whom you see the Spirit come down and remain is he who will baptize with the Holy Spirit" – **John 1:33**.

In his Gospel, Luke concludes the testimony of John the Baptist concerning Jesus saying:

"When all the people were being baptized, Jesus was baptized too. And as he was praying, heaven was opened, and the Holy Spirit descended on him in bodily form like a dove" – **Luke 3:21 – 22**.

Luke continues:

"Jesus, full of the Holy Spirit, returned from the Jordan and was led by the Spirit into the desert. Jesus returned to Galilee in the power of the Spirit, and news about him spread through the whole countryside" – **Luke 4:1, 14.**

Moreover, Luke emphasizes Jesus' command to His disciples:

"Do not leave Jerusalem, but wait for the gift my Father promised, which you have heard me speak about. But you will receive power when the Holy Spirit comes on you; and you will be my witness in Jerusalem, and in all Judea and Samaria, and to the ends of the earth" – **Acts 1:4, 8.**

Oswald J. Smith explains that "the purpose of the Spirit's fullness is for the bestowal of power." He is of the opinion that no carnal person can wage war against sin and win without the power of the Holy Spirit. There is no country that would send its army to fight without proper equipment; in the same vein, Spirit-filled life is necessary for fruitful Christian service. Thus, Smith concludes that "the fullness of the Spirit is the Christian warrior's equipment for service." The subject of baptism in the Holy Spirit is one of the most valued Christian doctrines in the New Testament Church.

Over the years, my teaching seminar sessions and personal experiences indicate that baptism in the Holy Spirit is the gift of the Father and is the necessary power for proclaiming the Gospel of Jesus Christ to the ends of the earth. The rationale for these teaching seminars is to "increase the knowledge of baptism in the Holy Spirit" because, firstly, many believers have lost their passion for witnessing and serving God in many Churches. Secondly, there is a lack of knowledge of baptism in the Holy Spirit among Church members. Thirdly, the decrease in knowledge of baptism in the Holy Spirit is due to a lack of teaching seminars on this vital aspect of the body of Christ. It is of utmost importance that Church pastors and leaders begin teaching seminars to increase the knowledge of the baptism in the Holy Spirit among their members and to empower them to be able to proclaim the Gospel in their communities and around the world.

It is time that Churches understand that without the baptism of the Holy Spirit in believers in a Church, the Church will not be able to achieve the Great Commission that Jesus Christ commanded before His ascension to heaven. In fact, this is one of the greatest challenges many Churches face. Many Christians pursue the "American dream" with vigor, with less regard for the "Kingdom of God dream". As a result, most members of the body of Christ continue to backslide in witnessing the Gospel and simply keep recycling members without any new converts joining the Churches for years. Thus, in many Churches, evangelical missions and outreaches have ceased to exist.

In addition to the fact that evangelism is less effective

in many Churches, much of the preaching and praying have centered more on spiritual warfare, the works of the enemy, career pursuits, daily bread, and prosperity, but not on winning souls to God's Kingdom. I strongly believe that a Church that does not evangelize or witness Christ anymore will become irrelevant in Christ, in their community, nation, and the world. Hence, I encourage Churches to seek the power of God through increasing knowledge of baptism in the Holy Spirit to become effective and relevant in witnessing the Gospel of Christ on earth. To be able to achieve this, the teaching seminars should continue regularly, and the lessons should be practical-oriented and relevant to the believer's appreciation of Spirit-empowerment for witnessing the Gospel of Christ. Every member whose knowledge of the baptism in the Holy Spirit is increased will benefit the Church and become more effective in whatever task God has given to him or her in the ministry.

Several arguments and opinions have evolved among several denominations about baptism in the Holy Spirit. Nevertheless, reading through some of the passages mentioned above, it will be observed that baptism in the Holy Spirit is connected with the Spirit of God in the life of a person who has received salvation through Christ. Thus, salvation in Christ becomes impossible without the indwelling of the Holy Spirit in the life of a person. In the passages discussed, baptism in the Holy Spirit is connected to prayer. In other words, prayer is one of the steps toward receiving the baptism in the Holy Spirit. Additionally, the purpose of waiting in the upper room, as commanded by Jesus to His disciples, was to "receive power" from above to be able to witness Christ to the ends of the earth; thus, every believer ought to be baptized in the Holy Spirit to achieve meaningful results in the Kingdom of God and become productive witnesses of Christ.

*How to Receive the Baptism in the Holy Spirit

Here are some more steps to receiving the baptism in the Holy Spirit. These steps are only guidelines, but God has different ways to empower His Church.

- **Ask Jesus the Spirit-baptizer Himself:** To receive the baptism in the Holy Spirit, those who desire to be baptized in the Holy Spirit should ask God (Luke 11:13).

- **Repentance:** On the Day of Pentecost, Apostle Peter called his listeners to repent and be baptized in the name of Jesus Christ (Acts 2:38).

- **Study, honor, and act on the Word of God:** Honoring God and acting on God's Word are requirements for believers to receive baptism in the Holy Spirit (Luke 11:11 – 13).

- **Assurance of salvation in Christ:** For those who desire to be baptized in the Holy Spirit, they must have first received salvation in Christ and confess

Jesus as their Lord and Savior. After salvation, believers need to demonstrate their love for God and man (Matthew 25:34 – 36; Luke 10:30 – 37; Romans 1:16; 8:31 – 32; 10:9, 10; 1 Corinthians 2:2; 2 Corinthians 5:14; Phillipians 1:20; 1 Thessalonians 2:1-12).

- **Laying on of hands:** Through the laying on of hands by men of God, a believer could be baptized in the Holy Spirit and begin to speak with new tongues (Acts 19:6).

- **Believe it is for you, desire it, and accept it as a gift of the Holy Spirit:** The Holy Spirit has been given already to the Church on the Day of Pentecost. It is the gift of the Father from above, and you cannot buy it with money nor do anything to earn it (John 7:37-39; Acts 2:38-39; Galatians 3:2, 5, 14).

- **You must receive water baptism through immersion:** The Bible records that Jesus, our example, was also baptized and immersed in the water by John the Baptist before being baptized in the Holy Spirit (Acts 10:47).

- **Yield, thirst, and surrender to God:** For seekers of baptism in the Holy Spirit, they must yield to God, be obedient to God – "total surrender to the will of God" because disobedience will hinder us from receiving the gift (Acts 5:38). Also, there is a need for the believers to thirst and desire for Holy Spirit baptism, but the desire must also be "pure" and not "selfish" (Luke 11:13).

- **Faith, prayer, and asking other believers to pray for you:** Through personal prayer and asking other believers to pray for you specifically to receive the baptism of the Holy Spirit, a believer can receive it by faith.

One of the attributes of God is power (Psalm 147:5). Luke emphasized the concept of Spirit and power in the earthly ministry of Jesus (Acts 10:38). In the book of Acts, the supernatural power of God is seen in operation through baptism in the Holy Spirit in the lives of the disciples (Acts 2:14 – 41, 42 – 47). This apostolic power was a result of the experience of baptism in the Holy Spirit on the Day of Pentecost. For centuries, God, in diverse ways, has continued to manifest Himself to the world through His deeds, His words, His power, and His works of creation. There is something unique and fundamental when God calls a believer to witness the Gospel of Jesus Christ to the ends of the earth; God will always equip those whom He calls to join Him in His redemptive plan to save the world (Exodus 4:10 – 12). In truth, witnessing the Gospel of Jesus Christ is an enormous task, and it is accomplished with spiritual warfare. The Bible records several examples of satanic powers obstructing God's redemptive mission for the world (Ephesians. 2:2; 6:10 – 11; Mark 5:1 – 11; cf. Luke 8:26 – 33; Acts 8:9 – 20; 2 Corinthians 4:3 – 4). At every encounter, God always reigns supreme over all the forces of the enemy.

"Then Jesus came to them and said, 'All authority in heaven and on earth has been given to me. Therefore go and make disciples of all nations, baptizing them in the name of the Father and of the Son and of the Holy Spirit, and teaching them to obey everything I have commanded you. And surely, I am with you always, to the very end of the age." – **Matthew 28:18 – 20**

Furthermore, believers must see the importance of spiritual gifts as embedded in the baptism of the Holy Spirit – spiritual gifts cannot be given or received without the power of the Holy Spirit. The scripture records that "When He ascended on high, He led captives in His train and gave gifts to men" (Ephesians 4:8). Jesus ascended by the power of the Holy Spirit, who also raised Him from the dead. Without the power of the Holy Spirit, nothing meaningful can be done in the kingdom. After being baptized in the Holy Spirit, Jesus began to manifest the gift of healing sick people (Luke 8:43 – 50; Mark 5:25 – 36). Surely, the baptism in the Holy Spirit is non-negotiable for effective witnessing of the Gospel of Christ to the ends of the earth (Romans 8:19 – 23). Apostle Paul affirms that only those who are led by the Spirit of the Lord will bring hope to the world. To bring hope to the world through witnessing the Gospel could only be possible through baptism in the Holy Spirit and through Spirit-empowerment accompanied by the manifestation of spiritual gifts of the Holy Spirit.

The application of the intent of Paul's statement is that

the Spirit of God is behind the Word of God. No one can speak, teach, or preach the Word of God or witness the Gospel productively without being baptized in the Holy Spirit. There is always a demonstration of power when the Word of God is spoken under the anointing of the Holy Spirit. Before witnessing can be effective, the Word of God must be supplied through the Holy Spirit to the speaker because persuasive words of humans will only produce emptiness in the ears of the listeners unless the words are Spirit-empowered. I daresay, the deficiency today in our twenty-first-century teaching and preaching ministries is a result of a lack of baptism in the Holy Spirit.

In conclusion, Thomson K. Mathew declares that the uniqueness of Pentecostal "preaching of the Gospel" is that it proceeds from the anointing of the Holy Spirit. Therefore, "It is preaching about Jesus in the power of the Holy Spirit." Mathew explains, "Simply put, Pentecostal preaching is preaching by a person filled with the Holy Spirit". This is the crux of the matter in witnessing the Gospel of Jesus to the ends of the earth; it is done through power from on high – the power of the Holy Spirit.

WORKBOOK
– Questionaire

Instruction:

Please check the appropriate answer for the following questions.

- **Definition, Meaning, Need, and Purpose of Baptism in the Holy Spirit**

1. I have heard about the Baptism in the Holy Spirit.
a. Strongly Agree ( )
b. Agree ( )
c. Disagree ( )
d. Strongly Disagree ( )

2. The Baptism in the Holy Spirit is the promise of the Father, and power from on high for every believer to witness the Gospel of Christ.
a. Strongly Agree ( )
b. Agree ( )
c. Disagree ( )
d. Strongly Disagree ( )

3. I have received the baptism in the Holy Spirit.
a. Strongly Disagree ( )
b. Disagree ( )
c. Strongly Agree ( )
d. Agree ( )

4. Through speaking in new tongues, I know I have been baptized in the Holy Spirit.

a. Strongly Disagree (   )
b. Disagree (   )
c. Strongly Agree (   )
d. Agree (   )

• **The Need for Baptism in the Holy Spirit**

5. A believer needs Baptism in the Holy Spirit to be like Jesus the Master.
a. Strongly Disagree (   )
b. Disagree (   )
c. Strongly Agree (   )
d. Agree (   )

6.   All the believers in the body of Christ need the Baptism in the Holy Spirit.
a. Strongly Disagree (   )
b. Disagree (   )
c. Strongly Agree (   )
d. Agree (   )

• **The Purpose of the Baptism in the Holy Spirit**

7. The purpose of Baptism in the Holy Spirit is for believers to receive power from above to be able to witness the Gospel of Jesus Christ to the ends of the earth.
a. Agree (   )
b. Disagree (   )
c. Strongly Disagree (   )
d. Strongly Agree (   )

8. Every believer will receive power after the Holy Spirit comes upon them (Acts 1:8).
a. Strongly Agree (   )
b. Agree (   )
c. Strongly Disagree (   )
d. Disagree (   )

- **The initial evidence of Baptism in the Holy Spirit for believers**

9. After the Baptism in the Holy Spirit, the initial evidence that follows is speaking in new tongues.
a. Strongly Disagree (   )
b. Strongly Agree (   )
c. Agree (   )
d. Disagree (   )

10. I believe in speaking in new tongues after a believer is baptized in the Holy Spirit.
a. Disagree (   )
b. Agree (   )
c. Strongly Disagree (   )
d. Strongly Agree (   )

- **The purpose of speaking in tongues**

11. One of the purposes of speaking in new tongues is for the edification of the body of Christ, which is the Church.
a. Strongly Disagree (   )
b. Disagree (   )

c. Strongly Agree ( )

d. Agree ( )

12. When someone is speaking in new tongues publicly in the Church, Apostle Paul taught that there should be an interpreter in the Church (1 Corinthians 14:9).

a. Strongly Disagree ( )

b. Disagree ( )

c. Strongly Agree ( )

d. Agree ( )

13. At times, it is possible for someone speaking in tongues to speak contrary to the Bible.

a. Strongly Disagree ( )

b. Disagree ( )

c. Agree ( )

d. Strongly Agree ( )

14. A believer can receive the baptism in the Holy Spirit without speaking in tongues.

a. Agree ( )

b. Strongly Agree ( )

c. Disagree ( )

d. Strongly Disagree ( )

• **Paul asked the two disciples he met at Ephesus: Did you receive the Holy Spirit when you believed? (Acts 19:2)**

15. Many believers in Christ have not received the Baptism in the Holy Spirit after receiving salvation in Christ.
a. Disagree (   )
b. Strongly Disagree (   )
c. Strongly Agree (   )
d. Agree (   )

16. Due to lack of knowledge, desire, and asking God in prayers, many believers in my Church have not received the Baptism in the Holy Spirit or heard about it.
a. Strongly Disagree (   )
b. Disagree (   )
c. Strongly Agree (   )
d. Agree (   )

- **Steps towards receiving Baptism in the Holy Spirit and the result**

17. Some of the steps towards receiving the baptism in the Holy Spirit are repentance, desire, asking God in faith, and studying the Word of God.
a. Agree (   )
b. Strongly Agree (   )
c. Strongly Disagree (   )
d. Disagree (   )

18. As a result of being baptized in the Holy Spirit, Church members will begin to grow in faith, be Spirit-empowered to witness, pray, preach, and stir revival to occur.

a. Agree ( )

b. Strongly Agree ( )

c. Strongly Disagree ( )

d. Disagree ( )

- **Baptism in the Holy Spirit and Gifts of the Holy Spirit**

19. In addition, after being baptized in the Holy Spirit, the believer will begin to manifest the gifts of the Holy Spirit, which will make them more effective in witnessing the gospel.

a. Strongly Agree ( )

b. Agree ( )

c. Strongly Disagree ( )

d. Disagree ( )

20. Being baptized in the Holy Spirit, I have been able to identify my spiritual gifts.

a. Strongly Agree ( )

b. Agree ( )

c. Strongly Disagree ( )

d. Disagree ( )

21. The gifts and move of the Holy Spirit will propel a Church revival in the 21st century.

a. Strongly Agree ( )

b. Agree ( )

c. Strongly Disagree ( )

d. Disagree ( )

22. Every seeker of Baptism in the Holy Spirit needs to tarry in prayer to receive Baptism in the Holy Spirit.
a. Strongly Disagree ( )
b. Disagree ( )
c. Strongly Agree ( )
d. Agree ( )

23. Out of the nine gifts of the Holy Spirit, the gifts of prophecy, healing, discernment, and working of miracle are the most popular spiritual gifts in the 21st century Church.
a. Strongly Disagree ( )
b. Disagree ( )
c. Agree ( )
d. Strongly Agree ( )

24. Out of the nine gifts of the Holy Spirit, the gifts of prophecy, healing, discernment, and working of miracle are the most misused spiritual gifts in the 21st Church.
a. Strongly Disagree ( )
b. Disagree ( )
c. Agree ( )
d. Strongly Agree ( )

25. After being baptized in the Holy Spirit, it is necessary for believers to remain Spirit-empowered and continue to witness the Gospel of Christ beginning from their local community to the ends of the earth.

a. Strongly Agree ( )
b. Agree ( )
c. Strongly Disagree ( )
d. Disagree ( )

Bibliography

Abodunde, Ayodeji. *A Heritage Faith*. Lagos, Nigeria: Pierce Watershed, 2017.

Anderson, Allan. *An Introduction to Pentecostalism: Global Charismatic Christianity*. New York: Cambridge Press, 2004.

Anderson, Robert Mapes. "Pentecostal and Charismatic Christianity." *The Encyclopedia of Religion. Vol. 11*. Edited by Mircea Eliade. New York: Macmillan, 1987. 229-235.

Arrington, French L. *Encountering the Holy Spirit: Paths of Christian Growth and Service*. Cleveland, TN: Pathway Press, 2003.

Bartleman, Frank. Azusa Street. South Plainfield, NJ: Bridge Publishing, 1980. Quoted in Allan Anderson, *An Introduction to Pentecostalism: Global Charismatic Christianity*, 36, n. 24. New York: Cambridge Press, 2004.

Basham, Don. *A Handbook on Holy Spirit Baptism*. New Kensington, PA: Whitaker House Publisher, 1973.

Beasley-Murray, G. R. *Baptism in the New Testament*. Grand Rapids, MI: Eerdmans, 1990.

Bock, Darrell L. *A Theology of Luke and Acts*. Grand Rapids: Zondervan, 2012.

Bonnke, Reinhard. *Evangelism by Fire*. Lake Mary, FL: Charisma House, 2011.

_____. *Holy Spirit: Revelation and Revolution; Exploring Holy Spirit Dimensions*. Orlando: E. R. Productions LLC, 2007.

Brueggemann, Walter. R*everberations of Faith: A Theological Handbook of Old Testament Themes*. Louisville: Westminster John Knox Press, 2002.

Bruner, Frederick Dale. *A Theology of the Holy Spirit: The Pentecostal Experience in the New Testament*. Eugene, OR: Wipf and Stock, 1970.

Burgess, Stanley M., ed. *Christian Peoples of the Spirit: A Documentary History Pentecostal Spirituality from the Early Church to the Present*. New York: New York University, 2011.

_____. "Holy Spirit, Doctrine of: The Medieval Churches." *The New International Dictionary of Pentecostal and Charismatic Movements*. Rev. ed. Edited by Stanley M. Burgess. Grand Rapids: Zondervan, 2002. 746-763.

_____. "Holy Spirit, Doctrine of: Reformation Traditions." *The New International Dictionary of Pentecostal and Charismatic Movements*. Rev. ed. Edited by Stanley M. Burgess. Grand Rapids: Zondervan, 2002. 763-769.

Calvin, John. *Calvin Commentaries*. Vol. 36. Acts, Part 1. Translated by John King. On Sacred-texts.com. N.d.

https://www.sacred-texts.com/chr/calvin/cc36/cc36016. htm (10 March 2018).

Cho, David Yonggi. *The Holy Spirit, My Senior Partner: Understanding the Holy Spirit and His Gifts.* Lake Mary, FL: Charisma House, 1989.

Cho, Youngmo. *Spirit and Kingdom in the Writings of Luke and Paul: An Attempt to Reconcile These Concepts.* Eugene, OR: Wipf and Stock, 2005.

Chrysostom, St. John. *Commentary on Hebrews 6:1-2.* Quoted in Randy Clark, *Baptized in the Holy Spirit: God's Presence Resting Upon You with Power.* 76, n. 19. Shippensburg, PA: Destiny Image Publishers, 2017.

Clark, Randy. *Baptized in the Holy Spirit: God's Presence Resting Upon You with Power.* Shippensburg, PA: Destiny Image Publishers, 2017.

Criswell, W. A. *The Baptism, Filling and Gifts of the Holy Spirit.* Grand Rapids, MI: Zondervan, 1973.

Del Colle, Ralph. *Christ and the Spirit: Spirit-Christology in Trinitarian Perspective.* New York: Oxford University Press, 1994.

_____. "Spirit Baptism: A Catholic Perspective." *In Perspectives on Spirit Baptism: Five Views,* ed. Chad Owen Brand, 241-290. Nashville: Broadman & Holman, 2004.

Dieter, Melvin E. "The Wesleyan Perspective." *In Five Views on Sanctification,* ed. Stanley N. Gundry, 9-58. Grand Rapids: Zondervan, 1987.

Dorries, David W. "Edward Irving and the 'Standing Sign' of Spirit Baptism." *In Initial Evidence: Historical and Biblical Perspectives on the Pentecostal Doctrine of Spirit Baptism,* ed. Gary B. McGee, 41-56. Eugene, OR: Wipf & Stock, 1991.

_____. *Spirit-Filled Christology: Merging Theology and Power.* San Diego: Aventine, 2006.

Douglas, J. D., and Merrill C. Tenney, eds. *The NIV Compact Dictionary of the Bible.* Grand Rapids: Zondervan, 1989.

Dunn, James D. G. *Baptism in the Holy Spirit: A Re-examination of the New Testament Teaching on the Gift of the Spirit in Relation to Pentecostalism Today.* London: SCM Press, 1970. Quoted in Max Turner, "The Work of the Holy Spirit in Luke-Acts," Word & World 23, no. 2 (Spring 2003): 147, n. 4. https://wordandworld. luthersem.edu/content/pdfs/23-2_Holy_Spirit /23-2_Turner.pdf (19 August 2018).

Dunning, H. Ray. "A Wesleyan Perspective on Spirit Baptism." *In Perspectives on Spirit Baptism: Five Views,* ed. Chad Owen Brand, 181-240. Nashville: Broadman & Holman, 2004.

Easton, Matthew George. *Easton's Bible Dictionary.* On

Biblestudytools.com. N.d. https://www.biblestudytools. com/dictionary/mahaneh-dan (10 September 2018).

Ervin, Howard M. *Conversion-Initiation and the Baptism in the Holy Spirit: An Engaging Critique of James D.G. Dunn's Baptism in the Holy Spirit.* Peabody, MA: Hendrickson, 1984.

_____. Spirit Baptism: *A Biblical Investigation.* Peabody, MA: Hendrickson, 1987.

_____. *These are Not Drunken as Ye Suppose.* Plainfield, NJ: Logos, 1968.

Fee, Gordon D. *Paul, the Spirit and the People of God* (Peabody, MA: Hendrickson Publishers, 1996), 149. Quoted in Michael Stafford Baynes Reid, "The Impact of Teaching the Peniel Model of Spiritual Warfare to Pastors," 72, n. 114. D.Min, proj., Oral Roberts University, 2002.

FGBMFI. *Five Questions Answered on Baptism in the Holy Spirit and Glossolalia.* Los Angeles: Full Gospel Business Men's Fellowship International, n.d.

Forbes, James. *The Holy Spirit and Preaching.* Nashville: Abingdon, 1989.

Foskett, Mary. "Annunciation." *The New Interpreter's Dictionary of the Bible.* Vol. 1. Edited by Katharine Doob Sakenfeld. Nashville: Abingdon Press. 165.

Gelpi, Donald L. ``Conversion: The Challenge of

Contemporary Charismatic Piety." *In The Reasoning Heart: Toward a North American Theology.* Edited by Frank Oppenheim. Washington DC: Georgetown University Press, 1984. Quoted in Koo Don Yun, *Baptism in the Holy Spirit: An Ecumenical Theology of Spirit Baptism.* 91, n. 29. Lanham, MD: University Press of America, 2003.

Gordon, M. R. *"Regeneration." The New Bible Dictionary.* *2nd ed.* Edited by N. Hillyer. Wheaton, IL: Tyndale House, 1982. 1015-1016.

Graham, Billy. *The Holy Spirit: Activating God's Power in Your Life.* Waco, TX: Word Books, 1978.

Gray, George Buchanan. *A Critical and Exegetical Commentary on Numbers.* The International Critical Commentary. Edinburgh: T. & T. Clark, 1903.

Grimm, Harold J. *The Reformation Era: 1500-1650.* New York: Macmillan, 1954.

Hagin, Kenneth E. *Baptism in the Holy Spirit.* Tulsa, OK: Kenneth Hagin Ministries, 2006.

Haldane, Robert. *A Commentary on the Epistle to the Romans* (London: The Banner of Truth Trust, 1960), 513. Quoted in Michael Stafford Baynes Reid, "The Impact of Teaching the Peniel Model of Spiritual Warfare to Pastors," 63, n. 76. D.Min, proj., Oral Roberts University, 2002.

Hart, Larry. "Responses to Stanley M. Horton's Pentecostal

Perspective: Response by Larry Hart." *In Perspectives on Spirit Baptism: Five Views,* ed. Chad Owen Brand, 94-96. Nashville: Broadman & Holman, 2004.

_____. "Spirit Baptism." I*n Spirit-Empowered Christianity in the 21st Century,* ed. Vinson Synan, 261-286. Lake Mary, FL: Charisma House, 2011.

_____. "Spirit Baptism: A Dimensional Charismatic Perspective." *In Perspectives on Spirit Baptism: Five Views,* ed. Chad Owen Brand, 105-180. Nashville: Broadman & Holman, 2004.

Hawthorne, Gerald F. *The Presence and the Power: The Significance of the Holy Spirit in the Life and Ministry of Jesus.* Eugene, OR: Wipf and Stock Publisher, 1991.

Hoekema, Anthony. *Holy Spirit Baptism.* Grand Rapids, MI: Eerdmans, 1972.

Horton, Michael. *The Christian Faith: A Systematic Theology for Pilgrims on the Way.* Grand Rapids: Zondervan, 2011.

Horton, Stanley M. "The Pentecostal Perspective." *In Five Views on Sanctification,* ed. Stanley N. Gundry, 103-148. Grand Rapids: Zondervan, 1987.

_____. "Responses to Ralph Del Colle's Catholic Perspective: Response by Stanley M. Horton." *In Perspectives on Spirit Baptism: Five Views,* ed. Chad Owen Brand,

286-287. Nashville: Broadman & Holman, 2004.

_____. "Spirit Baptism: A Pentecostal Perspective." *In Perspectives on Spirit Baptism: Five Views*, ed. Chad Owen Brand, 47-104. Nashville: Broadman & Holman, 2004.

Hudson, Neil. "Strange Words and Their Impact on Early Pentecostals—A Historical Perspective." *In Speaking in Tongues: Multi-Disciplinary Perspectives*, ed. Mark J. Cartledge, 52-80. Milton, Keynes, UK: Paternoster Press, 2006.

Irving, Edward. *Edward Irving's Holy Spirit Writings*. Edited by David W. Dorries. North Charleston, SC: David Dorries, 2011.

Jules-Rosette, Bennetta. "African Religion: Modern Movements." *The Encyclopedia of Religion. Vol. 1.* Edited by Mircea Eliade. New York: Macmillan, 1987. 82-89.

Kaiser, Walter C., Jr. "The Baptism in the Holy Spirit as the Promise of the Father: A Reformed Perspective." *In Perspectives on Spirit Baptism: Five Views*, ed. Chad Owen Brand, 15-46. Nashville: Broadman & Holman, 2004.

_____. "The Pentateuch." In *A Biblical Theology of the Holy Spirit*, ed. Trevor J. Burke and Keith Warrington, 1-11. Eugene, OR: Cascade Books, 2014.

Kane, J. Herbert. *Christian Missions in Biblical Perspective* (Grand Rapids, MI: Baker, 1976), 65. Quoted in Solomon

Uche Ashibuogwu, "Increasing the Knowledge of Evangelism among International Groups." 12, n. 2. D.Min. proj., Oral Roberts University, 2012.

Keener, Craig S. Acts: *An Exegetical Commentary.* Vol. 1. Grand Rapids: Baker Academic, 2012.

Land, Steven Jack. *A Passion for the Kingdom: An Analysis and Revision of Pentecostal Spirituality.* Ann Arbor, MI: Emory University, 1991.

Lederle, Henry I. *Theology with Spirit: The Future of the Pentecostal and Charismatic Movements in the 21st Century* (Tulsa, OK: Word & Spirit Press, 2010), 172, ebook, 281, n. 45. Quoted in Randy Clark, Baptized in The Holy Spirit: God's Presence Resting Upon You with Power, 46, n. 12. Shippensburg, PA: Destiny Image Publishers, 2017.

Lindsay, Gordon, and Freda Lindsay. *21 Reasons Why Christians Should Speak in Tongues.* Dallas: Christ for the Nations, 2004.

Loveday, Alexander. *Acts in Its Ancient Literary Context.* London: T & T Clark, 2005. Quoted in Caleb Opoku Nyanni, "Spirit Baptism and Power: Luke's Concept of Spirit and Power Reflected in The Church of Pentecost with Specific References to the Church of Pentecost in Birmingham, England," 20, n. 41. Master's thesis, University of Manchester, 2014.

Macchia, Frank D. "Babel and the Tongues of Pentecost: Reversal or Fulfilment? A Theological Perspective." In *Speaking in Tongues: Multi-Disciplinary Perspectives*, ed. Mark J. Cartledge, 34-51. Milton, Keynes, UK: Paternoster Press, 2006.

_____. *Baptized in the Spirit: A Global Pentecostal Theology* (Grand Rapids, MI: Zondervan, 2006), 60. Quoted in Randy Clark, Baptized in The Holy Spirit: God's Presence Resting Upon You with Power, 45, n. 11. Shippensburg, PA: Destiny Image Publishers, 2017.

Mathew, Thomson K. *Spirit-Led Ministry in the 21st Century.* Maitland, FL: Xulon, 2004.

McDonnell, Kilian, ed. *Presence, Power, Praise* (Collegeville, MN: The Liturgical Press, 1980), 13-15. Quoted in Koo Dong Yun, *Baptism in the Holy Spirit: An Ecumenical Theology of Spirit Baptism*, 46-47, n. 3. Lanham, MD: University Press of America, 2003.

McGrath, Alister E. *Christian Theology: An Introduction.* 5th ed. London: Wiley-Blackwell, 2011.

Menzies, Robert P. *Empowered for Witness: The Spirit in Luke and Acts.* Sheffield: Sheffield Academic, 1994.

Metz, Donald S. *Speaking in Tongues: An Analysis.* Kansas City, MO: Nazarene Publishing House, 1964.

Munroe, Myles. *The Most Important Person on Earth:*

The Holy Spirit, Governor of the Kingdom. New Kensington, PA: Whitaker House, 1991.

Nolland, *John. Luke 1–9:20.* Word Biblical Commentary. Vol. 35A. Dallas: Word Books, 1989.

Olowe, Abi. *Great Revivals Great Revivalist: Joseph Ayo Babalola.* Houston: Omega Publishers, 2007.

Otis, George, Jr. *Informed Intercession: Transforming Your Community through Spiritual Mapping and Strategic Prayer* (Ventura, CA: Renew Books, 1999), 85. Quoted in Michael Stafford Baynes Reid, "The Impact of Teaching the Peniel Model of Spiritual Warfare to Pastors," 25, n. 64. D.Min, proj., Oral Roberts University, 2002.

Oyedepo, David O. *Commanding the Supernatural.* Lagos, Nig.: Dominion Publishing House, 2006.

_____. *The Mandate: Operational Manual of Living Faith Church Worldwide.* Lagos, Nig.: Dominion Publishing House, 2012.

_____. *Manifestations of the Spirit: Unveiling the Seven Spirits of God.* Lagos, Nig.: Dominion Publishing House, 1997.

_____. *The Release of Power.* Lagos, Nig.: Dominion Publishing House, 1996.

Peel, John David Yeadon. *Aladura: A Religious Movement*

among the Yoruba. London: Oxford University Press for International African Institute, 1968.

Peters, Albrecht. "Sanctification: Dogmatics." *The Encyclopedia of Christianity.* Vol. 4. Translated and edited by Geoffrey W. Bromiley. Grand Rapids, MI: Eerdmans, 2005. 840-842.

Pinnock, Clark H. Flame of Love: *A Theology of the Holy Spirit.* Downers Grove, IL: InterVarsity Press, 1996.

Polhill, John B. Acts. The New American Commentary. Vol. 26. Nashville: Broadman & Holman, 1992.

Rea, John. *The Holy Spirit in the Bible: All the Major Passages About the Spirit; A Commentary.* Lake Mary, FL: Creation House, 1990.

Robeck, Cecil M., Jr. *The Azusa Street Revival and Mission: The Birth of the Global Pentecostal Movement.* Nashville: Thomas Nelson, 2006.

Roberts, Oral. *The Baptism with the Holy Spirit and the Value of Speaking in Tongues Today.* Tulsa, OK: Oral Roberts, 1969.

_____. *The Holy Spirit in the Now* I. Tulsa, OK: Oral Roberts University, 1974. https://digitalshowcase.oru. edu/cgi/viewcontent.cgi?article=1012& context=holyspiritnow (7 July 2019).

Sanders, J. Oswald. *The Holy Spirit and His Gifts.*

Grand Rapids, MI: Zondervan, 1970.

Schaff, Philip. *History of the Christian Church*. Vol. 1. Apostolic Christianity, A.D. 1-100. On Christian Classics Ethereal Library. N.d. http://www.ccel.org/ccel/ schaff/hcc1.pdf (10 February 2019).

Shank, David. "African Independent Churches." In *Christianity in Today's World,* ed. Robin Keeley, 144-148. Grand Rapids, MI: Eerdmans, 1985.

Simpson, A. B. *The Holy Spirit, or Power from on High*. Camp Hill, PA: Christian Publications, 1896.

Smith, Oswald J. *The Enduement of Power*. London: Marshall, Morgan & Scott, 1962.

Spurgeon, Charles H. *Sermons Preached by C. H. Spurgeon. Revised and Published During the Year 1908*. In The Metropolitan Tabernacle Pulpit (Pasadena, TX: Pilgrim Publications, 1978), 54:342-43. Quoted in Michael Stafford Baynes Reid, "The Impact of Teaching the Peniel Model of Spiritual Warfare to Pastors," 71, n. 106. D.Min, proj., Oral Roberts University, 2002.

Stolz, Fritz. "Sanctification: OT." *The Encyclopedia of Christianity,* Vol. 4. Translated and edited by Geoffrey W. Bromiley. Grand Rapids, MI: Eerdmans, 2005. 839.

Synan, Vinson. "The Charismatic Renewal after Fifty Years." In *Spirit-Empowered Christianity in the 21st Century,* ed. Vinson Synan, 7-24. Lake Mary, FL: Charisma House, 2011.

Torrey, R. A. *The Baptism with the Holy Spirit.* Minneapolis: Bethany House, 1972.

_____. *Torrey on Prayer.* Compiled and edited by Beverlee J. Chadwick. Alachua, FL: Bridge-Logos, 2009.

Turner, Max. "Early Christian Experience and Theology of 'Tongues'—A New Testament Perspective." In *Speaking in Tongues: Multi-Disciplinary Perspectives,* ed. Mark J. Cartledge, 1-33. Milton, Keynes, UK: Paternoster Press, 2006.

Tyra, Gary. *The Holy Spirit in Mission: Prophetic Speech and Action in Christian Witness.* Downers Grove, IL: IVP Academic, 2011.

Ukachi, Austen C. *The Best is Yet to Come: Pentecostal and Charismatic Revivals in Nigeria 1914-1990s.* Lagos, Nig.: Summit Press, 2013.

Ukah, Azonzeh F. K. *A New Paradigm of Pentecostal Power: A Study of the Redeemed Christian Church of God in Nigeria.* Trenton, NJ: Africa World Press, 2008.

Walvoord, John F. "The Augustinian-Dispensational Perspective." In *Five Views on Sanctification,* ed. Stanley N. Gundry, 197-283. Grand Rapids: Zondervan, 1987.

Warfield, Benjamin B. *Biblical and Theological Studies.* Grand Rapids: Baker, 1968.

_____. *The Person and Work of the Holy Spirit.* Amityville, NY: Calvary Press, 1997.

Warrington, Keith. "The Synoptic Gospels." In *A Biblical Theology of the Holy Spirit,* ed. Trevor J. Burke and Keith Warrington, 84-103. Eugene, OR: Cascade Books, 2014.

Waterhouse, Steven. *Not By Bread Alone: An Outlined Guide to Bible Doctrine.* Amarillo, TX: Westcliff, 2007.

Winslow, Octavius. *The Work of the Holy Spirit: An Experimental and Practical View.* Edinburgh: Banner of Truth Trust, 2013.

Yun, Koo Dong. *Baptism in the Holy Spirit: An Ecumenical Theology of Spirit Baptism.* Lanham, MD: University Press of America, 2003.